THE PHILOSOPHY
OF ACTION

Edited by
ALAN R. WHITE

OXFORD UNIVERSITY PRESS

Oxford University Press

OXFORD LONDON NEW YORK
GLASGOW TORONTO MELBOURNE WELLINGTON
CAPE TOWN SALISBURY IBADAN NAIROBI DAR ES SALAAM LUSAKA ADDIS ABABA
BOMBAY CALCUTTA MADRAS KARACHI LAHORE DACCA
KUALA LUMPUR SINGAPORE HONG KONG TOKYO

FILMSET BY ST PAUL'S PRESS, MALTA
PRINTED IN GREAT BRITAIN
AT THE UNIVERSITY PRESS, OXFORD
BY VIVIAN RIDLER
PRINTER TO THE UNIVERSITY

F11

CONTENTS

ACKNOWLEDGEMENTS

I am indebted to my colleagues, Mr. Roger Montague, Mr. Richard Swinburne and Dr. Christopher Williams, and to the Editor of the Series, Mr. G. J. Warnock, for their criticisms of an earlier draft of my Introduction. My thanks are also due to many friends, and especially Mr. Roland Hall, who gave me suggestions both for articles in the collection and for items in the bibliography. Random House Inc. have generously permitted me to re-use in the Introduction some material from Chapter 6 of my recent book *The Philosophy of Mind*.

A. R. W.

INTRODUCTION

PHILOLOGISTS until quite recently followed Plato (Sophist 261–2) in defining a verb as 'a sign expressive of an action' (cp. Palmer 33).[1] An act, say jurisprudents (cp. Dias 17, ch. 10), is 'the foundation of legal liability'; though this dictum neglects the importance of omissions. For psychology and sociology, action is behaviour orientated towards a goal (cp. Parsons and Shils 34; Taylor 8). The important philosophical questions about action concern its nature, its description and its explanation.

A. *The nature of action*

Philosophers sometimes use 'do', 'action', and 'act' indifferently, but in ordinary language these are words of decreasing scope. Not everything one does, much less everything one is accountable for, is an action or an act.

'Do' may function either as an auxiliary, e.g. 'Did he go? I do not know', or as a stand-in for various other verbs, e.g. 'If he wants to eat or drink or rest, let him do so'. As an auxiliary, its use seems unrestricted. 'Do (did) you **X**?' can be answered by using any verb, e.g. 'eat', 'belong', 'deserve', 'hope', 'intend', 'see', 'discover', 'fall', 'try', 'omit'. As a stand-in, 'do' is more limited. It can be substituted, indeed, for any episodic verb, including not only acts, actions and activities (e.g. 'kill', 'move', 'work'), but also accomplishments (e.g. 'discover'), happenings (e.g. 'fall'), ways of passing the time (e.g. 'sleep'), attempts and omissions. It cannot, however, stand in for states (e.g. 'doubt'), tendencies (e.g. 'despise'), possessions (e.g. 'know'), and many other things (e.g. 'belong', 'mean', 'intend', 'deserve', etc.). None of these is something we 'do'.

'Action' is commonly used to point a contrast between a state of movement and a state of quiescence, between action and inaction, activity and inactivity. Action is something we may make ready for or take, something we may be sent or galvanised into or be put out of, something which may be instant or delayed. We contrast seeing a person and seeing him in action. 'Action' sometimes indicates a contrast between the apparently quiescent state of the thinker and

[1]References are either to the numbered items of the bibliography, e.g. Melden 5, or to items reprinted in this collection, e.g. MELDEN.

the overt movements of the man of action or between the man who only talks and the man who gets things moving. We contrast action with thought and actions with words. Natural or manufactured objects, like the heart, chemical agents, the planets or engines, have an action, which may be slow, complicated or beautiful; but they do not take action, they do not act, however much they may act on other things.

To act is to take action. An act is the taking of action. Contrast 'his first or last act', 'caught in the act' with 'course of action', 'effective action'. An act is not a species of action (e.g. D'Arcy 1, p. 7; contrast Sachs 39). There are acts, but not actions, of mercy and desperation; smooth and beautiful actions, but not acts. Attempts are acts, but omissions are not. In trying to do X there must be some act or acts the doing of which constitutes the attempt; in omitting to do X there need not be, and usually is not, any act.

There is no good reason to suppose (e.g. AUSTIN, p. 21; Baier 13, pp. 183–9) that the philosophical notions of *act* and *action* are much, if at all, different from those expressed in ordinary language. A difference is certainly not shown by the fact (e.g. Baier) that a man who can properly be described in ordinary language as 'doing nothing' (i.e. nothing important, effective, relevant, illegal) may yet be performing what a philosopher might call 'an action'; for in ordinary language too such a man may also be described as 'doing something' (e.g. lazing about, talking when action is needed, etc.). Philosophers who have supposed that verbs like 'know', 'believe', 'intend', 'mean', signify mental acts have been making a logical mistake; they have not been introducing a philosophical sense of 'act'. Furthermore, philosophers have sometimes given criteria for 'an action' which are really criteria for 'a human action', e.g. in terms of intention, purpose or consciousness (e.g. Baier 13), and criteria for 'a human action' which are really criteria for 'a voluntary action', e.g. in terms of will, volition, choice (e.g. Hobbes 23; Austin 11; Holmes 24; etc.). It is, therefore, worthwhile indicating the features common to all actions.

To act is to bring about something, to cause it to happen; an action is the bringing about of something. An agent or author is that which brings something about. Things may be brought about either directly or by means of other things (e.g. Danto 15; Chisholm 14). We make the table move by extending our leg, but we don't make our leg extend by doing something else, such as moving our muscles. Moving one's muscles by or in extending one's leg is not the same as extending one's leg by or in moving one's muscles; although whichever we do has the same results (e.g. Melden 5, ch. 6). But, though we can distinguish what we cause directly and what we cause by some means, it is misleading to say that we do not cause the former at all (e.g. Danto 15, pp. 439–41; DANTO, pp. 44–6; contrast Chisholm 14) or that the former is what we 'do' and the latter what we 'make happen' (e.g. Ladd 28). In fact what we 'do' covers both our bringing something about, directly or indirectly (e.g. move our leg or move the table), and our achievement of a result (e.g. discover, solve), while 'act' and 'action' refer to the former. The action of light bleaches cotton, but the bleaching effect of light is not an action of the light. The successes we chalk up are things we do, yet they are not actions we take. Furthermore, not every change produced is a detachable product of something prior, as a cake is a product of baking (e.g. Ladd 28). We produce a smile in smiling and words in talking, whereas we may produce happiness by smiling and astonishment by talking. Nor need every change be known to the agent. It does not follow that I have not done X just because I did not realize, or did not intend, in doing Y that I would bring X about (e.g. MELDEN).

To attribute or ascribe an act or action to something or someone, therefore, is to call him or it the author or cause of what is brought about; it is to say that he brought the happening about (cp. Locke 29; MacMurray 30; Chisholm 14; Baier 12; Kenny 4, ch. 8; contrast PRICHARD; MELDEN; Melden 5, pp. 23–25, 43; Ladd 28). A human action is an action whose author is a human being; but reference to the equipment, whether purpose, intention or motive, of such an author should not appear in the analysis of *action*.

Since, however, it is human action that particularly interests lawyers, psychologists and philosophers, I shall limit my survey to analyses of that.

(*a*) Any attempt to analyse *action* (or *act* or *deed*) as simply that which is expressed by a verb is mistaken. As Locke pointed out, 'what is signified by verbs that grammarians call active does not always signify action' (29, II.xxi. 74; cp. MacMurray 30, p. 71). They may signify a state ('believe', 'doubt', 'expect'), a tendency ('despise', 'want'), a possession ('have', 'know'), an acquisition ('find', 'arrive', 'realize'), a happening ('fall', 'tremble'). Much of contemporary analytic philosophy, like that of Aristotle (e.g. 1048b 18–35, 1094a 4–5, 1140a 1–17, 1173a 31–1174b 5), has been devoted to categorizing the different kinds of concepts signified by verbs (e.g. Ryle 38, ch. 5; Vendler 43; Kenny 4, chs. 7–8; Potts 37; Taylor 41); though the

Aristotelian labels (e.g. 1048b 18–35) of 'kinesis', 'energeia', 'praxis' and 'poiesis' do not signify divisions of events into actions and non-actions. There are, for instance, both kineseis (e.g. become, be moved) and energeiai (e.g. understand, be happy) which are not actions, as well as kineseis (build) and energeiai (listen) which are actions (cp. Kenny 4; Potts 37; Taylor 41; Ackrill 9). Linguistic differences, such as transitive/intransitive (e.g. I shook my head/I shook with fear), active/passive (e.g. I crushed it/I was crushed by it) or alternative forms (e.g. jump/fall, raise/rise), are clues to the existence of a logical difference between action and happening. But they are by no means infallible clues; nor do they tell us the nature of the difference between, e.g. 'I raise my arm' and 'My arm rises'.

(b) A recent analysis of *action* (Hart 22; contrast FEINBERG, Geach 20, Pitcher 36) argues that to say that X is a human action is not to describe anything that happened but to 'ascribe responsibility' for it. But to this there are several objections.

First, Hart does not distinguish between the action we take and the deed we do. He takes 'A did X' as the expression of an action. But, as we have seen, our successes count among our deeds but not among our actions. Nor does he always distinguish carefully enough between being responsible for a happening, e.g. damage to a window, and being responsible for one's action in bringing about a happening, e.g. breaking a window. Though this is not to deny (as Pitcher 36, pp. 227–9; Ladd 28) that one can be responsible for an action as well as a happening. We often plead for a person beside himself with grief or hatred that he isn't responsible for what he is saying or doing. Nor does the ascription of responsibility serve to distinguish human action from the action of a physical object, for we can as properly say, without any trace of animism, that the wind is responsible for the damage to the window as that a person is responsible for it.

Secondly, 'A is responsible for X' and 'A did X' cannot mean the same; for there are several kinds of things for which a man can now be responsible, but which are not things that he has done or even that he could have done, as when a man is responsible for what may happen or for ensuring either that it does or does not happen or for what other people cause to happen. Even where what A is responsible for and what A did are the same, e.g. damage to a window, to say that A is responsible for the damage is not the same as saying A did the damage; for A could be responsible for it, even if someone else did it, and could do it without being held responsible. At most, A's doing X might be sufficient to make him responsible for X. The question whether A did X is a straightforward causal question; but the question whether A is responsible for X may depend on the existence of some rule or undertaking in virtue of which he has the responsibility for what has happened. Although many philosophers (e.g. FEINBERG, p. 104; Pitcher 36; contrast Pennock 35) have wrongly held that 'responsible for' sometimes simply means 'cause of', this cannot be Hart's view, since his analysis of 'A did X' is meant to contradict those who hold 'the natural view that to ascribe an act to an agent is a causal description of the act' (Geach 20).

(c) The commonest analyses of *action* have characterized it in terms of an alleged antecedent.

1. Traditionally the presence of such an antecedent has been made a *necessary* condition of something's being an action, and this antecedent has been called 'the will'. The nineteenth-century jurisprudent J. Austin expressed this tradition thus: 'Certain movements of our bodies follow invariably and immediately our wishes and desires for the same movements . . . These antecedent wishes and these consequent movements are human *volitions* and *acts* (strictly and properly so called) . . . Our desires of those bodily movements which immediately follow our desires for them are the only *volitions*; or (if you prefer the expression better) the only acts of the will... ' (11, lect. XVIII). But the idea that a human act (or action) is a bodily movement following from or caused by the will, a volition or an act of will, occurs earlier in Hobbes (23, 1.6), Locke (29, II.xxi), Hume (25, II.iii.1; cp. 26, §vii) and Mill (31, III.v.11) and remained dominant in nineteenth-century and early twentieth-century philosophy (cp. the quotations from James, Stout, Cook Wilson in PRICHARD; cp. Ewing 18); though, as PRICHARD points out, there was some ambiguity as to whether what we are supposed to will are actions or happenings. This view has also been accepted by most analytic jurisprudents after Austin (cp. Holmes 24; Dias 17). It has, however, several difficulties.

In the first place, it fails or refuses to distinguish between an act and a voluntary act. Austin (cp. Hobbes and Holmes) said 'A voluntary movement of my body, or a movement which follows a volition, is an act'; and some contemporary philosophers and jurisprudents (e.g. Ryle 38, p. 74; Williams 45, ch.I; Dias 17, p. 252) have called a 'nonvoluntary act' a self-contradiction. Now, if we assume that an act is necessarily a voluntary act, the conclusion that an act is something necessarily preceded by a volition is more seductive because it relies on the plausible-sounding premise that a voluntary act is necessarily something preceded by a volition. But neither this assumption nor this premise is correct.

The assumption that all acts are voluntary confuses the objection that something is not a voluntary act because it is not an act at all and the objection that something is not a voluntary act because it is a non-voluntary (or obligatory) act. Men can do things or have things done to them; they can do things voluntarily or do them because they are obliged to do them. The contrast between a voluntary and an obligatory subscription or resignation is a contrast between two things I do, the one voluntarily and the other obligatorily. But the contrast between a subscription and a levy, or between a resignation and a dismissal, is a contrast between what I do and what is done to me. What I do, thinking I am obliged to do it, I do not voluntarily do, since I do it thinking I have to do it. What is done to me I do not voluntarily do, since I do not do it at all.

The premise that a voluntary act is something preceded by a volition or act of will is also incorrect. For, besides the objections, mentioned below, which it shares with the general thesis that an act is something preceded by a volition, it is based on a false analysis of the notion of *voluntary*.

To do x voluntarily is to do x with the awareness that one has an alternative course open to one. What I do non-voluntarily I do because I am obliged to do it, that is, because in the circumstances all alternatives other than X are closed to me either physically—these are the cases discussed by FITZGERALD—legally, morally, or in some other way. If what I do is unintentional, unknowing, or in certain ways non-attentive, then, though it is still an act of mine, it is neither voluntary nor obliged, since it is not done in the knowledge either that there is or that there is not a choice (contrast Anscombe 48, p. 398).

The view that an act or action itself is something, e.g. a bodily movement, preceded or caused by the will (or a volition) also has well-known difficulties clearly set out by MELDEN (cp. Ryle 38, ch. 3; Wittgenstein 46, §§611ff.; Vesey 44; Pears 7, ch. 2). These are: (i) the difficulty of characterizing the alleged volition itself, despite the traditional assertion (e.g. Locke 29, II. xxi; Hume 25, II. iii. 1; Mill 31, III.v.11; PRICHARD) that everyone is clearly conscious of it. It does not, for instance, have the qualities of an act (cp. Ryle 38; MELDEN), nor can it properly be regarded as an instrument (cp. Wittgenstein 46, §§614, 616; Melden 5, chs. 4–5; Danto 15) with which movements are made, nor (pace MacIntyre 77) was it, or can it properly be, identified with resolution, decision, intention, etc.; (ii) the difficulty of characterizing the relation between the volition and the bodily movement which follows it, for this seems to be at the same time both logical and causal (cp. MELDEN; contrast DAVIDSON).

2. Attempts (e.g. Ewing 18, pp. 93–94; Taylor 8, ch. 2) to characterize an action in terms of a contingent rather than a necessary antecedent, e.g. in terms of some effort of will, resolution, intention, decision, purpose, aim etc., must be unsuccessful. First, because it is on this view always logically possible that an act be performed without such an antecedent; hence, the nature of an act is still unclarified. Secondly, because experience clearly shows that actions often lack such an antecedent. We often do things without any effort of will, without resolving or deliberating whether to do them, unintentionally, nonvoluntarily, for no purpose, etc. Thirdly, because such a view often misconstrues such factors as decision and intention as prior processes which cause our movements (e.g. MacIntyre 77, pp. 224–5). Fourthly, because such factors cannot transform a bodily happening into an action, since what they can properly be said to precede are actions, not happenings.

(d) Instead of saying that human actions are happenings with certain necessary or contingent antecedents, it is often suggested that such actions are events or occurrences which it makes sense to qualify in certain ways. We can, for instance, intend, try, choose, decide, be ordered, resolve or refuse to *jump*, but not to *fall*; to *smile* or *move*, but not to *ache*, to *deserve*, to *mean* or to *know*. We can jump, but not fall, impulsively, deliberately, intentionally, automatically, thoughtlessly, unwittingly or reluctantly. We have the power or the ability to jump, but not to fall (e.g. Hampshire 3, ch. 1). We can fall, but not jump, without knowing or thinking that we are doing so. One knows, when one does know, whether one jumped in a different way from that in which one knows whether one fell (cp. Anscombe 58; Hampshire 3, ch. 3). One can predict either that one will jump or that one will fall; one can, however, intend only to jump, not to fall. It makes sense to ask 'How did you know you were falling?', but not 'How did you know you were jumping?'

We can have a reason or purpose for jumping, or moving, but not for falling, or deserving. We can jump, but not fall, voluntarily or involuntarily. A shop-keeper can raise his prices voluntarily or be obliged to raise them, but his prices can only happen to or be bound to rise. We are praised or blamed for our actions, but envied or pitied either for our successes and failures or for what happened to us. Both actions and happenings may be good or bad, but only actions can be right or wrong.

None of this shows, of course, that human actions must be voluntary, intentional, purposive, conscious, etc. (pace Ewing 18, p. 93; Franks 19, pp. 113–20; Taylor 8, pp. 27ff.); but only that they must be the sorts of occurrences of which it makes sense to ask whether they are any or all of these. Furthermore, these qualifications provide criteria for distinguishing human actions both from non-human actions and from non-actions; they do not tell us what the difference is. Nor, indeed, do they distinguish between an act and its omission. They do not turn occurrences into actions, for they presuppose that what is thus qualified is an action. They apply to human actions because they give the qualities of human agents. When what is made to happen is made so by a human being, then these qualities are appropriate.

A particular happening is an action if it is the exercise of a power to make that happen (cp. Melden 5, chs. 4 and 7; Hampshire 3). It may be such a power that Locke and others meant when they talked about the will (e.g. Locke 29; Austin 11, lect. XVIII). Human beings and animals gradually acquire various powers over their own limbs and thoughts; not by learning what means or instrument to use, but directly. If we acquire the ability to wink an eye or waggle an ear, we are not in a position to tell how it is done, nor to teach others, but only to do it.

These acquired powers may be exercised on occasion automatically, by reflex, impulsively, without paying attention or unconsciously. Or they may be exercised deliberately, intentionally, voluntarily or for a purpose. They may be exercised from inclination, desire or resolution; they may be exercised effortlessly or only with strength of body and will. We can, in addition, learn to make other things happen by learning *how* to make them, that is, what means to adopt, as when we learn how to annoy a colleague or how to start a car.

B. *Descriptions of Action*

There is no description which is *the* description of a given act or action any more than there is *the* description of an object or event; though many descriptions of it will be definitely wrong (cp. D'Arcy 1, ch.1).

Given that what happens is a human act, that is, that it is something brought about by a human being, we can, for instance, describe it in physical terms, e.g. moving an arm, or by its agent, e.g. the act of a madman or a gentleman, or as being of a certain kind, whether moral, e.g. act of charity or injustice, or psychological, e.g. act of desperation or kindness, or legal, e.g. act of bigamy or perjury, or institutional, e.g. act of homage or loyalty. In order to qualify for one of these descriptions the event must, in addition to being something that is brought about, meet certain criteria in morals, the law, etc.; though these criteria are not mentioned in the description (cp. Anscombe 47). An act may be described in explanatory terms by reference to its purpose, reason or cause, e.g. practising the piano, obeying an order, an act of stupidity. Its description may contain a reference to its circumstances, e.g. its time (burglary is stealing between certain hours) or manner (slouching, mumbling) or its conventions (cheating, castling) or the relation of the agent to the person affected (an act of piety is confined to one in a filial relation, rape is intercourse without consent with someone other than one's wife); or to its consequences, e.g. homicide is an attack whose result is the death of the victim within a year and a day, saving a person's life is different from merely pulling him out of the water; or to some antecedent event, e.g. repetition, volleying; or to an intention, e.g. stalking, an act of fraud; or to some motive, e.g. an act of jealousy or greed; or to its object, e.g. treason is an act against the state, stealing is taking other people's property.

Jurisprudents, following Bentham and Austin (Austin 11, lect. XVIII; cp. Dias 17, ch. 10) reduce all descriptions of acts to three classes, namely 'acts proper' (the basic physical movement of the agent, such as pulling the trigger of a gun), 'acts and circumstances' (trespass, perjury, bigamy) and 'acts and consequences' (assault, battery, homicide). In a parallel way J. L. Austin (49) classed all speech-acts as either locutions—that is, uttering meaningful words—or illocutions—that is, doing something in uttering these words e.g. warning, advising, proclaiming—or perlocutions—that is, achieving something by uttering these words, e.g. convincing, persuading, intimidating. Aristotle (N.E., 1111a 1–24) reduced the relevant circumstances of action to six and Bentham (52, ch. vii, para. 27) to three.

The description given to an act or action is important for several reasons. First, since two acts may be the same in regard to some features and different in regard to others, they may share one description and not another. Thus, two acts may be properly described as 'crossing the boundary', but only one as 'trespassing', since only it is without the owner's consent. Further, while both are the same because they are boundary crossings, they may differ in physical movements, time, place and manner. Similarly, the one act may be susceptible of various different, though not contradictory, descriptions according as reference is or is not made to a particular feature. It is, therefore, important to specify the act as 'an act of . . .' (e.g. mercy, murder, negligence, etc.). This does not mean, however, that language is changing the world or that we are neglecting the world in favour of language (e.g. Bennett 64) or that our procedure is arbitrary (e.g. Ladd 28, p. 643). For we can properly give a different description only because we are taking account of some different feature. To speak of 'different descriptions of the same act' or of 'the same action X being intentional under one description Y and not under another Z' can be misleading.

Secondly, *in* doing one thing, e.g. signing my name, or *by* doing one thing, e.g. making a noise, I may do another, e.g. issue a proclamation or annoy my neighbour. Such cases are central to Ryle's polymorphous concepts and mongrel-categorical statements (38, pp. 135–49) and Austin's illocutionary and perlocutionary speech-acts (49) and underlie Anscombe's and Melden's analyses of intentional act (Anscombe 58, §§23–26; Melden 5, ch.9). Here we can say *either* that there is only one act, e.g. signing my name or making a noise, which amounts to or results in something else, e.g. the issue of a proclamation or the annoyance of my neighbour, and which can, therefore, have two descriptions, *or* that there are two acts, e.g. signing my name (making a noise) and issuing a proclamation (annoying my neighbour). The reasons for saying that there are two acts are that I could both intend to do and do one without the other, and that there are features present in the second act which are absent from the first. On the other hand, there are not two acts in the way that there are two acts when e.g. I sign my name and shake hands. For, I can say that in or by signing my name, I thereby issue a proclamation, whereas I cannot say that in or by signing my name, I thereby shake hands. Although 'signing my name' is no more synonymous with 'issuing a proclamation' than with 'shaking hands', I can say that signing *is*, in these circumstances, issuing a proclamation, whereas signing is not, in any circumstances, shaking hands. The former, but not the latter, pair may be 'photographically and gramophonically as similar as you please' (Ryle 38, p. 140). An answer to the question 'In doing what, was he Xing?' could be said to give a more 'fundamental' description of what was done than 'X' gives (cp. Anscombe 58, §47) and 'By doing what, was he Xing?' could be said to give a more 'basic' description (cp. DANTO). Under the 'basic', but not the 'fundamental', description, the act may be causally related to the Xing. It does not follow, however, that only fundamental or basic acts, such as muscular contractions, are acts properly so called (e.g. Austin 11, lects.XVIII–XIX; Holmes 24). Further, the less basic or less fundamental description may explain the act as it appears under the more elementary description; e.g. 'obeying an order' may both describe and explain what was described as 'signing my name'. An explanatory description may even mention the non-explanatory description, e.g. 'obediently signing my name'. The fact that an explanation of an action may take the form of a redescription of it does not entail anything about the type of explanation and, therefore, does not rule out a causal factor (as Melden 5, pp. 87–89; Taylor 8, pp. 36–37; contrast DAVIDSON). An act of killing may be described as an act of drunkenness or stupidity, that is, as something done because the agent was drunk or stupid, just as a dent in the woodwork may be described causally as a bullet hole or a mark in the sand as a footprint.

Thirdly, we can restrict the description of the action to some of its features—provided we retain the essential feature that it is the bringing about of something—and describe the other features separately as particular circumstances, e.g. the time, the manner, the antecedent, the consequences, the motive, etc. of the action.

One such restriction, common in morals, divides an act from its consequences (e.g. D'Arcy 1, ch. 1; Austin 11, lect. IX; Chopra 53; Griffin 55). There is, however, no incompatibility in describing something at one time as the consequences of an act, but at another time as part of the act. If the act is described in certain terms, e.g. making a noise, these other things that happened may be its consequences e.g. annoying a neighbour. But the act could have been described in the same case in such a way, e.g. as annoying a neighbour, as to make the consequences part of the act. The reason why some descriptions of consequences—and these are probably what are more commonly called consequences—cannot be descriptions of actions is that they are achievement-descriptions or result-descriptions, e.g. 'succeed', 'win', 'inherit', or 'become happy', 'be sacked'. We cannot ask someone for his reasons for doing these as we can ask him for his reasons for angering a neighbour, poisoning his wife or distracting the driver, any one of which may be a consequence of other actions. This has nothing to do with the moral significance or the unanticipatability of the consequences (e.g. D'Arcy 1, pp. 19–35; Anscombe 58, §§ 23–26). Nor can descriptions of the consequences properly be excluded from descriptions of the act on the grounds that an act is willed movement and consequences are never, or only some-

times, willed (e.g. Austin 11, lect. XIX) nor on the grounds that
an act must be intentional and that consequences are often unintentional. It is, indeed, not true that X cannot be said to be an act
or action of A unless A knew or intended it under that description
(e.g. Ewing 18, p. 93; Benson 51, p. 253; Beck 62, p. 169; Taylor
8, chs. 2–3; Meiland 56; DAVIDSON; contrast Will 57). What I do may
be the act of a madman, an act of bigamy or trespass, without my having the faintest idea that this is what I am doing. I can as easily shoot
the Prime Minister without knowing I am shooting the Prime
Minister as I can see the Prime Minister without realizing I see him.
This is not to deny that if a person is trying to do something, he must
know that he is; and must know this without inferring it from his
movements (cp. Hampshire 2). Nor is it to deny that *some* descriptions
of action are incorrect unless this action is known to the agent under
that description, e.g. to lie, to forge, to make a contract, to cheat;
for these descriptions refer, amongst other things, to the knowledge or
intention of the agent (cp. Anscombe 58, §47).

Finally, any assessment, whether legal, moral or of some other
kind, of an act depends on the description of the act, which, in turn,
depends on how much is assigned to the act and how much to its circumstances, consequences, etc. To pull someone out of the water may
be morally neutral, while to save his life may be praiseworthy. Murder
is abhorrent and illegal, but killing need be neither.

C. *Explanations of Action*

We need to distinguish, first, between explanations of human
actions and explanations of human happenings (e.g. blushing and
trembling), states (e.g. ignorance and expectation), feelings (e.g.
fear and suspicion), omissions, failings, etc.

Secondly, we need to distinguish within the wide variety of
explanations of human actions (e.g. White 85, ch.6). Some of this
variety shows itself in the colloquial phrases we may substitute
for the simple 'Why?' (cp. URMSON). We may ask for the purpose,
point or aim of what someone does; or what prompted, drove, persuaded or possessed him to do it. Further variety appears in the
generic words we have for the myriad factors occurring in explanations. These may be antecedent factors, as when a person's actions
are explainable by what he has at that very moment perceived, thought
or felt. A man may throw up his hands because he has just read a
congratulatory telegram or intervene in a conversation because he
felt a sudden inclination to do so. Or they may be law-like factors,

as when we explain behaviour by reference to habits, traits of character, or other kinds of disposition. Much of what we do is to be explained by our honesty, forgetfulness or indolence. Or they may be teleological factors, as in explanations by motive, desire, purpose and, sometimes, intention. We can also account for what someone does by reference to his state of mind, his attention or inattention, his knowledge or ignorance. A man may step on another's foot from carelessness or inadvertence or take another's umbrella intentionally or by mistake.

Finally, we need to distinguish between the different descriptions of the action to be explained. For, just as the identification of the action may influence our assessment of it, so it may limit the sorts of explanation applicable to it. For example, we can in a given instance describe what someone is doing either as playing the piano or as practising for a concert; but, while we can explain why he is playing the piano by saying that he is practising for a concert, we cannot explain why he is practising for a concert either by saying that he is playing the piano, or, of course, by simply repeating that he is practising for a concert. If by turning on the light I ruin your photographic plate, my reason for turning on the light, e.g. that I wanted to see where I was going, is not necessarily my reason, if I have one, for ruining your plate.

The great variety of explanations of human action leads to several questions. For instance, (i) How does each of these explanations actually explain? (ii) How are the different explanations, and the various factors that occur in each, related to each other? (iii) Are some of these kinds of explanations mutually exclusive? (iv) How many, if any, of these explanations give an explanation of a causal kind, or, if this is different, of the kinds which are found either in explanations of human characteristics other than behaviour or in explanations of inanimate nature? I have space here to give only a very few samples—and these deliberately controversial—of what I think are correct answers to these questions (cp. White 85, ch. 6).

(i) If we consider an explanation in terms of a motive, e.g. a desire to blacken a rival's character, we can show that such a motive is not an antecedent psychological occurrence, such as a feeling or thought (e.g. Hobbes 23; Hume 25; etc); nor is it a disposition to behave (e.g. Ryle 38, ch. iv); nor is it the intention to do the deed (e.g. ANSCOMBE; Melden 5, ch. 9).

The mere occurrence of a feeling or a thought is neither necessary nor sufficient to provide a motive for what I do. A man who works hard from ambition does not have ambitious feelings. Conversely, if I lash out because I am in pain or go to bed because I feel tired, I do not act from a motive. Greed, unaccompanied by any thought of a juicy steak, may be my motive for hurrying my morning's work; whereas the thought of the steak, which makes me smack my lips, does not give me a motive for smacking my lips.

Nor do dispositions necessarily provide motives. Timidity is not a motive for hesitating to answer, nor is tactlessness a motive for dropping conversational bricks. The fact that some dispositions, such as greed, vindictiveness and patriotism, undoubtedly do feature as motives is due, not to their being dispositions, but to their reference to action 'for the sake of' something further (e.g. Sutherland 83). Besides, a person can correctly be said to act from a motive even when he has no disposition to do what he did, as when I kill a man to prevent him revealing a secret.

Nor can intentions be properly quoted as motives for action. Motives, but not intentions, imply desires. An explanation in terms of what a person desires or wants to do is not the same as one in terms of what he intends to do. Furthermore, to cite a motive is necessarily to offer an explanation, whereas to mention an intention is not. If I go to Australia with the intention both of visiting my grandchildren and of returning to England before Christmas, the latter intention cannot be the explanation of my journey to Australia, even if the former can; whereas whatever is quoted as one of my motives for the journey must be part of the explanation. Motives imply desires. Avaricious men want possessions, and patriotic men want to serve their country. But desires do not necessarily imply motives. If a person does something just because he wants to do it, he does not act from a motive. Further, our desires, especially when unsatisfied, can make us rage and sulk, but we do not ordinarily rage and sulk from a motive. To give the motive for a deed is to indicate that desire for the sake of satisfying which the deed was done, provided that what was done was not itself the deed which was desired, but a deed which the agent thought would bring about or would amount to what was desired. The indication of such a desire may mention a specific desire, as when the desire to prevent someone from changing his will is the motive for murder; or it may mention the object desired, e.g. money or power; or it may mention one of those traits e.g. avarice, ambition, vindictiveness, or one of those emotions, e.g. jealousy or pity, which involves a desire for such and such.

(ii) Part of the answer to our second question 'How are the various explanations of actions related to each other?' should be clear from the previous answer. Here is an additional example.

What is the difference between saying that a man started to sing loudly in the corridor because he suddenly *felt inclined* to do so and saying that he started to sing because he *is inclined* to do so when he thinks he is alone? Though there is a natural relation between these two—for commonly we are inclined to do what we feel inclined to do and feel inclined to do what we are inclined to do—they are logically distinct. A man who is inclined to split his infinitives may never have felt inclined to do so, indeed may repudiate the suggestion that he does; while a man who often feels inclined to laugh at the mistakes of others may resolutely contain himself. A man may sing loudly in the corridor because he is inclined to forget that there are other people working in the building, but he could not feel inclined to forget this. The inclination of the person who 'feels inclined' to do something is akin to a temptation, whereas the inclination of the person who 'is inclined' to do or to suffer something is akin to a proneness. To feel indignant is to feel inclined to protest; to be tactless is to be inclined to drop conversational bricks. An explanation in terms of a proneness-inclination is like an explanation in terms of a trait. It refers to a law-like generalization about his conduct; it explains the behaviour in question as an instance of a type. An explanation in terms of a tempt-ation-inclination, on the other hand, makes no reference to a generalization; it may, indeed, mention some itch or impulse which we feel prior to what we do and because of which we do it. It suggests we are already falling over or bursting into doing it. Fear, indignation, interest and joy are typically things we are full of or even bursting with and, therefore, typically contain a felt-inclination to rush into action.

(iii) The answer to our third question is that some pairs of explan-ations are mutually compatible while others are mutually exclusive (cp. URMSON). There is, for instance, nothing incompatible about explaining a man's action both by a trait of character, e.g. vanity, and by a sudden temptation, e.g. to show off. We saw that there is often a natural connexion between a temptation-inclination and a proneness-inclination, and also that many character traits, like ambition, greed or patriotism, can be defined in terms of the kinds of motives with which they provide their possessors.

There is, on the other hand, an incompatibility between supposing that a man has done something merely as a reflex, from absent-mind-edness, carelessness or from pure force of habit and supposing that he can have done it from a motive (cp. Sutherland 83). Again, if we know he did something because he felt like doing it, we cannot sensibly ask him what was the point of his doing it. More disputably, if a man does something purely for pleasure, he cannot, I think, have done it either from a motive or for a purpose. To do it for pleasure is to do it simply for its own sake, whereas my earlier analysis of *motive* entailed that to do something from a motive is to do it for the sake of something else. Furthermore, the old hedonistic view that the pleasure of doing something is the purpose, indeed the only purpose, for which it is done rests on the dubious assumption that 'to do something for pleasure' is to be analysed analogously to 'to do something for money'. This assumption is dubious for the same sort of reason as the assumption that to acquire anything 'by luck' or 'by chance' is analogous to acquiring it by skill, hard work or the help of another. 'For pleasure' is used, I think, to indicate that there was no purpose for which or motive from which the deed was done; it was done simply for itself, because one wanted to do it; just as 'by luck' indicates that there was no assistance by which the result was acquired.

(iv) Our last problem—'How many, if any, explanations of human behaviour are of a causal kind?'—has had most of the limelight in recent discussions of explanations of human behaviour (e.g. MELDEN; DAVIDSON; ANSCOMBE; Hart and Honoré 71; Ayer 60; MacIntyre 76, 77; Hamlyn 70; Smart 82; Baier 61; Brandt 66). Its solution would depend on complete and detailed answers to the other three problems. Here I shall merely distinguish a few of the issues.

First, it must be emphasized how unsatisfactory the whole con-troversy is because of the vagueness of the idea of *cause*.

Secondly, it is explanations of *actions* that are in question, e.g. why the schoolboy broke the window or why the man raised his arm. The problem is whether any, or every, explanation of the schoolboy's breaking the window is of the same kind as any explanation of the window's breaking.

Thirdly, the kind of explanation offered by a person's reasons, that is, his desires, intentions, motives, beliefs etc., should be distinguished from those offered by other factors, such as environmental or heredit-ary conditions, drugs or drunkenness, the behaviour of other people, happenings in the world (e.g. flashes and noises) or the momentary feelings and perceptions of the agent himself (e.g. DAVIDSON; ANSCOMBE; Ayer 60; MacIntyre 77). The latter could be causal factors without the former being causal. Current controversy has in fact centred round the question whether, e.g., a schoolboy's reason for breaking the window explains his action exactly as the cause of the window's breaking explains that happening.

Philosophers who assimilate reasons to causes (e.g. DAVIDSON; Ayer 60; MacIntyre 77) have rightly pointed out certain similarities between the two kinds of explanation. Both the cause-explanation and the reason-explanation can be signified by the words 'because' and 'cause' and even 'reason'. Each explanation may on suitably described occasions give the necessary and/or sufficient conditions of the occurrence of what is to be explained. Generalizations may link reasons for actions and actions just as they link causes for happenings and happenings. Thus, dissatisfaction may lead to rebellion just as damp may cause disease. A happening, e.g. a bullet hole, may be described in terms which refer to its cause as easily as an act, e.g. of jealousy, may be described in terms of its reason.

Philosophers (e.g. MELDEN; ANSCOMBE; Hampshire 2, 3; Taylor 8, ch. 2;), who separate reasons and causes rightly emphasize their logical differences. The mere presence of the words 'because', 'cause' and 'but for' in two explanations does not make them of the same kind. A person's reason for doing X must contain a reference either to X or to something which is thought by the agent to be a means to X. It is in virtue of this characteristic, and not (e.g. Ayer 60; Hamlyn 70, p. 134) of any psychological or physiological characteristic, that a desire explains an action. In order for something to qualify as a cause, on the other hand, it must observe Hume's rule (25, I. iii. 12) that 'there is nothing in any object considered in itself which can afford us a reason for drawing a conclusion beyond it'. This rule has been interpreted by some (MELDEN; Beck 62, 63; contrast Goldberg 69) as meaning that an alleged cause must be describable without reference to its alleged effect. Furthermore, reasons, but not causes, can be good or bad, defensible or indefensible. One's reasons are known in a way that causes are not. Finally, if my curiosity to see what would happen can be said to have caused me to press a button and pressing a button caused the death of some people in a room, then my curiosity might be said to have caused their death; but though curiosity to see what happened was my reason for pressing the button, it was not my reason for killing the people (cp. Bennett 64).

Underlying much of the interest in reasons for actions is the query whether they are analogous to, reducible to or exclusive of the physio-logical causes of the bodily movements which partly constitute one's action. Is, for instance, the desire to give a good performance, which may be a pianist's reason for practising for a concert, identical or correlatable with some physiological element which causes the physical movements in which the practising is manifested? And could the physiological element which caused the physical movements also be said to have caused the action of practising for a concert? The objection to this view is that, however true its physiological assump-tions, an explanation by desire is not equivalent in meaning to an explanation by a physiological element, nor does what explains one item, e.g. the movements of one's fingers or even playing the piano, necessarily explain what that item may in the circumstances amount to, e.g., practising for a concert.

I

A PLEA FOR EXCUSES

J. L. Austin

THE subject of this paper, *Excuses*, is one not to be treated, but only to be introduced, within such limits. It is, or might be, the name of a whole branch, even a ramiculated branch, of philosophy, or at least of one fashion of philosophy. I shall try, therefore, first to state *what* the subject is, *why* it is worth studying, and *how* it may be studied, all this at a regrettably lofty level: and then I shall illustrate, in more congenial but desultory detail, some of the methods to be used, together with their limitations, and some of the unexpected results to be expected and lessons to be learned. Much, of course, of the amusement, and of the instruction, comes in drawing the coverts of the microglot, in hounding down the minutiae, and to this I can do no more here than incite you. But I owe it to the subject to say, that it has long afforded me what philosophy is so often thought, and made, barren of—the fun of discovery, the pleasures of co-operation, and the satisfaction of reaching agreement.

What, then, is the subject? I am here using the word 'excuses' *for a title*, but it would be unwise to freeze too fast to this one noun and its partner verb: indeed for some time I used to use 'extenuation' instead. Still, on the whole 'excuses' is probably the most central and embracing term in the field, although this includes others of importance—'plea', 'defence', 'justification' and so on. When, then, do we 'excuse' conduct, our own or somebody else's? When are 'excuses' proffered?

In general, the situation is one where someone is *accused* of having done something, or (if that will keep it any cleaner) where someone is *said* to have done something which is bad, wrong, inept, unwelcome, or in some other of the numerous possible ways untoward. Thereupon he, or someone on his behalf, will try to defend his conduct or to get him out of it.

One way of going about this is to admit flatly that he, X, did do that very thing, A, but to argue that it was a good thing, or the

From *Proceedings of the Aristotelian Society*, Vol. 57 (1956–7), pp. 1–30. Reprinted by courtesy of the Editor of the Aristotelian Society.

right or sensible thing, or a permissible thing to do, either in general or at least in the special circumstances of the occasion. To take this line is to *justify* the action, to give reasons for doing it: not to say, to brazen it out, to glory in it, or the like.

A different way of going about it is to admit that it wasn't a good thing to have done, but to argue that it is not quite fair or correct to say *baldly* 'X did A'. We may say it isn't fair just to say X did it; perhaps he was under somebody's influence, or was nudged. Or, it isn't fair to say baldly he *did* A; it may have been partly accidental, or an unintentional slip. Or, it isn't fair to say he did simply *A*—he was really doing something quite different and A was only incidental, or he was looking at the whole thing quite differently. Naturally these arguments can be combined or overlap or run into each other.

In the one defence, briefly, we accept responsibility but deny that it was bad: in the other, we admit that it was bad but don't accept full, or even any, responsibility.

By and large, justifications can be kept distinct from excuses, and I shall not be so anxious to talk about them because they have enjoyed more than their fair share of philosophical attention. But the two certainly can be confused, and can *seem* to go very near to each other, even if they do not perhaps actually do so. You dropped the tea-tray: Certainly, but an emotional storm was about to break out: or, Yes, but there was a wasp. In each case the defence, very soundly, insists on a fuller description of the event in its context; but the first is a justification, the second an excuse. Again, if the objection is to the use of such a dyslogistic verb as 'murdered', this may be on the ground that the killing was done in battle (justification) or on the ground that it was only accidental if reckless (excuse). It is arguable that we do not use the terms justification and excuse as carefully as we might; a miscellany of even less clear terms, such as 'extenuation', 'palliation', 'mitigation', hovers uneasily between partial justification and partial excuse; and when we plead, say, provocation, there is genuine uncertainty or ambiguity as to what we mean—is *he* partly responsible, because he roused a violent impulse or passion in me, so that it wasn't truly or merely me acting 'of my own accord' (excuse)? Or is it rather that, he having done me such injury, I was entitled to retaliate (justification)? Such doubts merely make it the more urgent to clear up the usage of these various terms. But that the defences I have for convenience labelled 'justification' and 'excuse' are in principle distinct can scarcely be doubted.

This then is the sort of situation we have to consider under 'excuses'. I will only further point out how very wide a field it covers. We have of course to bring in the opposite numbers of excuses—the expressions that *aggravate*, such as 'deliberately', 'on purpose' and so on, if only for the reason that an excuse often takes the form of a rebuttal of one of these. But we have also to bring in a large number of expressions which at first blush look not so much like excuses as like accusations—'clumsiness', 'tactlessness', 'thoughtlessness' and the like. Because it has always to be remembered that few excuses get us out of it *completely*: the average excuse, in a poor situation, gets us only out of the fire into the frying pan—but still, of course, any frying pan in a fire. If I have broken your dish or your romance, maybe the best defence I can find will be clumsiness.

Why, if this is what 'excuses' are, should we trouble to investigate them? It might be thought reason enough that their production has always bulked so large among human activities. But to moral philosophy in particular a study of them will contribute in special ways, both positively towards the development of a cautious, latter-day version of conduct, and negatively towards the correction of older and hastier theories.

In ethics we study, I suppose, the good and the bad, the right and the wrong, and this must be for the most part in some connexion with conduct or the doing of actions. Yet before we consider what actions are good or bad, right or wrong, it is proper to consider first what is meant by, and what not, and what is included under, and what not, the expression 'doing an action' or 'doing something'. These are expressions still too little examined on their own account and merits, just as the general notion of 'saying something' is still too lightly passed over in logic. There is indeed a vague and comforting idea in the background that, after all, in the last analysis, doing an action must come down to the making of physical movements with parts of the body; but this is about as true as that saying something must, in the last analysis, come down to making movements of the tongue.

The beginning of sense, not to say wisdom, is to realize that 'doing an action', as used in philosophy,[1] is a highly abstract expression—it is a stand-in used in the place of any (or almost any?) verb with a personal subject, in the same sort of way that 'thing' is a stand-in for any (or when we remember, almost any) noun substantive, and

[1] This use has little to do with the more down-to-earth occurrences of 'action' in ordinary speech.

'quality' a stand-in for the adjective. Nobody, to be sure, relies on such dummies quite implicitly quite indefinitely. Yet notoriously it is possible to arrive at, or to derive the idea for, an over-simplified metaphysics from the obsession with 'things' and their 'qualities'. In a similar way, less commonly recognized even in these semi-sophisticated times, we fall for the myth of the verb. We treat the expression 'doing an action' no longer as a stand-in for a verb with a personal subject, as which it has no doubt some uses, and might have more if the range of verbs were not left unspecified, but as a self-explanatory, ground-level description, one which brings adequately into the open the essential features of everything that comes, by simple inspection, under it. We scarcely notice even the most patent exceptions or difficulties (is to think something, or to say something, or to try to do something, to do an action?), any more than we fret, in the *ivresse des grandes profondeurs*, as to whether flames are things or events. So we come easily to think of our behaviour over any time, and of a life as a whole, as consisting in doing now action A, next action B, then action C, and so on, just as elsewhere we come to think of the world as consisting of this, that and the other substance or material thing, each with its properties. All 'actions' are, as actions (meaning what?), equal, composing a quarrel with striking a match, winning a war with sneezing: worse still, we assimilate them one and all to the supposedly most obvious and easy cases, such as posting letters or moving fingers, just as we assimilate all 'things' to horses or beds.

If we are to continue to use this expression in sober philosophy, we need to ask such questions as: Is to sneeze to do an action? Or is to breathe, or to see, or to checkmate, or each one of countless others? In short, for what range of verbs, as used on what occasions, is 'doing an action' a stand-in? What have they in common, and what do those excluded severally lack? Again we need to ask how we decide what is the correct name for 'the' action that somebody did—and what, indeed, are the rules for the use of 'the' action, 'an' action, 'one' action, a 'part' or 'phase' of an action and the like. Further, we need to realize that even the 'simplest' named actions are not so simple—certainly are not the mere makings of physical movements, and to ask what more, then, comes in (intentions? conventions?) and what does not (motives?), and what is the detail of the complicated internal machinery we use in 'acting'—the receipt of intelligence, the appreciation of the situation, the invocation of principles, the planning, the control of execution and the rest.

In two main ways the study of excuses can throw light on these fundamental matters. First, to examine excuses is to examine cases where there has been some abnormality or failure: and as so often, the abnormal will throw light on the normal, will help us to penetrate the blinding veil of ease and obviousness that hides the mechanisms of the natural successful act. It rapidly becomes plain that the breakdowns signalized by the various excuses are of radically different kinds, affecting different parts or stages of the machinery, which the excuses consequently pick out and sort out for us. Further, it emerges that not *every* slip-up occurs in connexion with *every*thing that could be called an 'action', that not every excuse is apt with every verb—far indeed from it: and this provides us with one means of introducing some classification into the vast miscellany of 'actions'. If we classify them according to the particular selection of breakdowns to which each is liable, this should assign them their places in some family group or groups of actions, or in some model of the machinery of acting.

In this sort of way, the philosophical study of conduct can get off to a positive fresh start. But by the way, and more negatively, a number of traditional cruces or mistakes in this field can be resolved or removed. First among these comes the problem of Freedom. While it has been the tradition to present this as the 'positive' term requiring elucidation, there is little doubt that to say we acted 'freely' (in the philosopher's use, which is only faintly related to the everyday use) is to say only that we acted *not* un-freely, in one or another of the many heterogeneous ways of so acting (under duress, or what not). Like 'real', 'free' is only used to rule out the suggestion of some or all of its recognized antitheses. As 'truth' is not a name for a characteristic of assertions, so 'freedom' is not a name for a characteristic of actions, but the name of a dimension in which actions are assessed. In examining all the ways in which each action may not be 'free', i.e., the cases in which it will not do to say simply 'X did A', we may hope to dispose of the problem of Freedom. Aristotle has often been chidden for talking about excuses or pleas and over-looking 'the real problem': in my own case, it was when I began to see the injustice of this charge that I first became interested in excuses.

There is much to be said for the view that, philosophical tradition apart, Responsibility would be a better candidate for the role here assigned to Freedom. If ordinary language is to be our guide, it is to evade responsibility, or full responsibility, that we most often make excuses, and I have used the word myself in this way above. But in fact 'responsibility' too seems not really apt in all cases: I do not exactly evade responsibility when I plead clumsiness or tactlessness, or, often, when I plead that I only did it unwillingly or reluctantly, and still less if I plead that I had in the circumstances no choice: here I was constrained and have an excuse (or justification), yet may accept responsibility. It may be, then, that at least two key terms, Freedom and Responsibility, are needed: the relation between them is not clear, and it may be hoped that the investigation of excuses will contribute towards its clarification.[1]

So much, then, for ways in which the study of excuses may throw light on ethics. But there are also reasons why it is an attractive subject methodologically, at least if we are to proceed from 'ordinary language', that is, by examining *what we should say when*, and so why and what we should mean by it. Perhaps this method, at least as *one* philosophical method, scarcely requires justification at present—too evidently, there is gold in them thar hills: more opportune would be a warning about the care and thoroughness needed if it is not to fall into disrepute. I will, however, justify it very briefly.

First, words are our tools, and, as a minimum, we should use clean tools: we should know what we mean and what we do not, and we must forearm ourselves against the traps that language sets us. Secondly, words are not (except in their own little corner) facts or things: we need therefore to prise them off the world, to hold them apart from and against it, so that we can realize their inadequacies and arbitrarinesses, and can re-look at the world without blinkers. Thirdly, and more hopefully, our common stock of words embodies all the distinctions men have found worth drawing, and the connexions they have found worth marking, in the lifetimes of many generations: these surely are likely to be more numerous, more sound, since they have stood up to the long test of the survival of the fittest, and more subtle, at least in all ordinary and reasonably

---

[1] Another well-flogged horse in these same stakes is Blame. At least two things seem confused together under this term. Sometimes when I blame X for doing A, say for breaking the vase, it is a question simply or mainly of my disapproval of A, breaking the vase, which unquestionably X did: but sometimes it is, rather, a question simply or mainly of how far I think X responsible for A, which unquestionably was bad. Hence if somebody says he blames me for something, I may answer by giving a *justification*, so that he will cease to disapprove of what I did, or else by giving an *excuse*, so that he will cease to hold me, at least entirely and in every way, responsible for doing it.

practical matters, than any that you or I are likely to think up in our armchairs of an afternoon—the most favoured alternative method.

In view of the prevalence of the slogan 'ordinary language', and of such names as 'linguistic' or 'analytic' philosophy or 'the analysis of language', one thing needs specially emphasizing to counter misunderstandings. When we examine what we should say when, what words we should use in what situations, we are looking again not *merely* at words (or 'meanings', whatever they may be) but also at the realities we use the words to talk about: we are using a sharpened awareness of words to sharpen our perception of, though not as the final arbiter of, the phenomena. For this reason I think it might be better to use, for this way of doing philosophy, some less misleading name than those given above—for instance, 'linguistic phenomenology', only that is rather a mouthful.

Using, then, such a method, it is plainly preferable to investigate a field where ordinary language is rich and subtle, as it is in the pressingly practical matter of Excuses, but certainly is not in the matter, say, of Time. At the same time we should prefer a field which is not too much trodden into bogs or tracks by traditional philosophy, for in that case even 'ordinary' language will often have become infected with the jargon of extinct theories, and our own prejudices too, as the upholders or imbibers of theoretical views, will be too readily, and often insensibly, engaged. Here too, Excuses form an admirable topic; we can discuss at least clumsiness, or absence of mind, or inconsiderateness, even spontaneousness, without remembering what Kant thought, and so progress by degrees even to discussing deliberation without for once remembering Aristotle or self-control without Plato. Granted that our subject is, as already claimed for it, neighbouring, analogous or germane in some way to some notorious centre of philosophical trouble, then, with these two further requirements satisfied, we should be certain of what we are after: a good site for *field work* in philosophy. Here at last we should be able to unfreeze, to loosen up and get going on agreeing about discoveries, however small, and on agreeing about how to reach agreement.[1] How much it is to be wished that similar field work will soon be undertaken in, say, aesthetics; if only we could forget for a while about the beautiful and get down instead to the dainty and the dumpy.

There are, I know, or are supposed to be, snags in 'linguistic'

[1]All of which was seen and claimed by Socrates, when he first betook himself to the way of Words.

philosophy, which those not very familiar with it find, sometimes not without glee or relief, daunting. But with snags, as with nettles, the thing to do is to grasp them—and to climb above them. I will mention two in particular, over which the study of excuses may help to encourage us. The first is the snag of Loose (or Divergent or Alternative) Usage; and the second the crux of the Last Word. Do we all say the same, and only the same, things in the same situations? Don't usages differ? And, Why should what we all ordinarily say be the only or the best or final way of putting it? Why should it even be true?

Well, people's usages do vary, and we do talk loosely, and we do say different things apparently indifferently. But first, not nearly as much as one would think. When we come down to cases, it transpires in the very great majority that what we had thought was our wanting to say different things of and in *the same* situation was really not so—we had simply imagined the situation *slightly* differently: which is all too easy to do, because of course no situation (and we are dealing with *imagined* situations) is ever 'completely' described. The more we imagine the situation in detail, with a background of story—and it is worth employing the most idiosyncratic or, sometimes, boring means to stimulate and to discipline our wretched imaginations—the less we find we disagree about what we should say. Nevertheless, *sometimes* we do ultimately disagree: sometimes we must allow a usage to be, though appalling, yet actual; sometimes we should genuinely use either or both of two different descriptions. But why should this daunt us? All that is happening is entirely explicable. If our usages disagree, then you use 'X' where I use 'Y', or more probably (and more intriguingly) your conceptual system is different from mine, though very likely it is at least equally consistent and serviceable: in short, we can find *why* we disagree—you choose to classify in one way, I in another. If the usage is loose, we can understand the temptation that leads to it, and the distinctions that it blurs: if there are 'alternative' descriptions, then the situation can be described or can be 'structured' in two ways, or perhaps it is one where, for current purposes, the two alternatives come down to the same. A disagreement as to what we should say is not to be shied off, but to be pounced upon: for the explanation of it can hardly fail to be illuminating. If we light on an electron that rotates the wrong way, that is a discovery, a portent to be followed up, not a reason for chucking physics: and by the same token, a genuinely loose or eccentric talker is a rare specimen to be prized.

As practice in learning to handle this bogey, in learning the essential *rubrics*, we could scarcely hope for a more promising exercise than the study of excuses. Here, surely, is just the sort of situation where people will say 'almost anything', because they are so flurried, or so anxious to get off. 'It was a mistake', 'It was an accident'—how readily these can *appear* indifferent, and even be used together. Yet, a story or two, and everybody will not merely agree that they are completely different, but even discover for himself what the difference is and what each means.[1]

Then, for the Last Word. Certainly ordinary language has no claim to be the last word, if there is such a thing. It embodies, indeed, something better than the metaphysics of the Stone Age, namely, as was said, the inherited experience and acumen of many generations of men. But then, that acumen has been concentrated primarily upon the practical business of life. If a distinction works well for practical purposes in ordinary life (no mean feat, for even ordinary life is full of hard cases), then there is sure to be something in it, it will not mark nothing: yet this is likely enough to be not the best way of arranging things if our interests are more extensive or intellectual than the ordinary. And again, that experience has been derived only from the sources available to ordinary men throughout most of civilized history: it has not been fed from the resources of the microscope and its successors. And it must be added too, that superstition and error and fantasy of all kinds do become incorporated in ordinary language and even sometimes stand up to the survival test (only, when they do, why should we not detect it?). Certainly, then, ordinary language is *not* the last word: in principle it can everywhere be supplemented and improved upon and superseded. Only remember, it *is* the *first* word.[2]

For this problem too the field of Excuses is a fruitful one. Here is a matter both contentious and practically important for everybody, so that ordinary language is on its toes: yet also, on its back it has long had a bigger flea to bite it, in the shape of the Law, and both again

---

[1] You have a donkey, so have I, and they graze in the same field. The day comes when I conceive a dislike for mine. I go to shoot it, draw a bead on it, fire: the brute falls in its tracks. I inspect the victim, and find to my horror that it is *your* donkey. I appear on your doorstep with the remains and say—what? 'I say, old sport, I'm awfully sorry, etc., I've shot your donkey *by accident*'? Or '*by mistake*'? Then again, I go to shoot my donkey as before, draw a bead on it, fire—but as I do so the beasts move, and to my horror yours falls. Again the scene on the doorstep—what do I say? 'By mistake'? Or 'by accident'?

[2] And forget, for once and for a while, that other curious question 'Is it true?' May we?

have lately attracted the attentions of yet another, and at least a healthily growing, flea, in the shape of psychology. In the law a constant stream of actual cases, more novel and more tortuous than the mere imagination could contrive, are brought up *for decision*—that is, formulae for docketing them must somehow be found. Hence it is necessary first to be careful with, but also to be brutal with, to torture, to fake and to override, ordinary language: we cannot here evade or forget the whole affair. (In ordinary life we dismiss the puzzles that crop up about time, but we cannot do that indefinitely in physics.) Psychology likewise produces novel cases, but it also produces new methods for bringing phenomena under observation and study: moreover, unlike the law, it has an unbiased interest in the totality of them and is unpressed for decision. Hence its own special and constant need to supplement, to revise and to supersede the classifications of both ordinary life and the law. We have, then, ample material for practice in learning to handle the bogey of the Last Word, however it should be handled.

Suppose, then, that we set out to investigate excuses, what are the methods and resources initially available? Our object is to imagine the varieties of situation in which we make excuses, and to examine the expressions used in making them. If we have a lively imagination, together perhaps with an ample experience of dereliction, we shall go far, only we need system: I do not know how many of you keep a list of the kinds of fool you make of yourselves. It is advisable to use systematic aids, of which there would appear to be three at least. I list them here in order of availability to the layman.

First we may use the dictionary—quite a concise one will do, but the use must be *thorough*. Two methods suggest themselves, both a little tedious, but repaying. One is to read the book through, listing all the words that seem relevant; this does not take as long as many suppose. The other is to start with a widish selection of obviously relevant terms, and to consult the dictionary under each: it will be found that, in the explanations of the various meanings of each, a surprising number of other terms occur, which are germane though of course not often synonymous. We then look up each of *these*, bringing in more for our bag from the 'definitions' given in each case; and when we have continued for a little, it will generally be found that the family circle begins to close, until ultimately it is complete and we come only upon repetitions. This method has the advantage of grouping the terms into convenient clusters—but of course a good deal will depend upon the comprehensiveness of our initial selection.

Working the dictionary, it is interesting to find that a high percentage of the terms connected with excuses prove to be *adverbs*, a type of word which has not enjoyed so large a share of the philosophical limelight as the noun, substantive or adjective, and the verb: this is natural because, as was said, the tenor of so many excuses is that I did it but only *in a way*, not just flatly like that—i.e., the verb needs modifying. Besides adverbs, however, there are other words of all kinds, including numerous abstract nouns, 'misconceptions', 'accident', 'purpose' and the like, and a few verbs too, which often hold key positions for the grouping of excuses into classes at a high level ('couldn't help', 'didn't mean to', 'didn't realize', or again 'intend' and 'attempt'). In connexion with the nouns another neglected class of words is prominent, namely, prepositions. Not merely does it matter considerably which preposition, often of several, is being used with a given substantive, but further the prepositions deserve study on their own account. For the question suggests itself, Why are the nouns in one group governed by 'under', in another by 'on', in yet another by 'by' or 'through' or 'from' or 'for' or 'with', and so on? It will be disappointing if there prove to be no good reasons for such groupings.

Our second source-book will naturally be the law. This will provide us with an immense miscellany of untoward cases, and also with a useful list of recognized pleas, together with a good deal of acute analysis of both. No one who tries this resource will long be in doubt, I think, that the common law, and in particular the law of tort, is the richest storehouse; crime and contract contribute some special additions of their own, but tort is altogether more comprehensive and more flexible. But even here, and still more with so old and hardened a branch of the law as crime, much caution is needed with the arguments of counsel and the dicta or decisions of judges: acute though these are, it has always to be remembered that, in legal cases—

(1) there is the overriding requirement that a decision be reached, and a relatively black or white decision—guilty or not guilty—for the plaintiff or for the defendant;

(2) there is the general requirement that the charge or action and the pleadings be brought under one or another of the heads and procedures that have come in the course of history to be accepted by the Courts. These, though fairly numerous, are still few and stereotyped in comparison with the accusations and defences of daily life. Moreover contentions of many kinds are beneath the law, as too

trivial, or outside it, as too purely moral,—for example, inconsiderateness;

   (3) there is the general requirement that we argue from and
abide by precedents. The value of this in the law is unquestionable,
but it can certainly lead to distortions of ordinary beliefs and
expressions.

For such reasons as these, obviously closely connected and stemming
from the nature and function of the law, practising lawyers and jurists
are by no means so careful as they might be to give to our ordinary
expressions their ordinary meanings and applications. There is
special pleading and evasion, stretching and strait-jacketing,
besides the invention of technical terms, or technical senses for
common terms. Nevertheless, it is a perpetual and salutary surprise to
discover how much is to be learned from the law; and it is to be added
that if a distinction drawn is a sound one, even though not yet
recognized in law, a lawyer can be relied upon to take note of it, for
it may be dangerous not to—if he does not, his opponent may.

   Finally, the third source-book is psychology, with which I include
such studies as anthropology and animal behaviour. Here I speak with
even more trepidation than about the Law. But this at least is clear,
that some varieties of behaviour, some ways of acting or explanations
of the doing of actions, are here noticed and classified which have not
been observed or named by ordinary men and hallowed by ordinary
language, though perhaps they often might have been so if they had
been of more practical importance. There is real danger in contempt
for the 'jargon' of psychology, at least when it sets out to supplement,
and at least sometimes when it sets out to supplant, the language of
ordinary life.

   With these sources, and with the aid of the imagination, it will
go hard if we cannot arrive at the meanings of large numbers of
expressions and at the understanding and classification of large
numbers of 'actions'. Then we shall comprehend clearly much that,
before, we only made use of *ad hoc*. Definition, I would add, explanatory definition, should stand high among our aims: it is not enough
to show how clever we are by showing how obscure everything is.
Clarity, too, I know, has been said to be not enough: but perhaps
it will be time to go into that when we are within measurable distance
of achieving clarity on some matter.

   So much for the cackle. It remains to make a few remarks, not, I
am afraid, in any very coherent order, about the types of significant

result to be obtained and the more general lessons to be learned from the study of Excuses.

(1) *No modification without aberration.*—When it is stated that X did A, there is a temptation to suppose that given some, indeed perhaps *any*, expression modifying the verb we shall be entitled to insert either it or its opppsite or negation in our statement: that is, we shall be entitled to ask, typically, 'Did X do A Mly or not Mly?' (e.g., 'Did X murder Y voluntarily or involuntarily?'), and to answer one or the other. Or as a minimum it is supposed that if X did A there must be at least *one* modifying expression that we could, justifiably and informatively, insert with the verb. In the great majority of cases of the use of the great majority of verbs ('murder' perhaps is not one of the majority) such suppositions are quite unjustified. The natural economy of language dictates that for the *standard* case covered by any normal verb,—not, perhaps, a verb of omen such as 'murder', but a verb like 'eat' or 'kick' or 'croquet'—no modifying expression is required or even permissible. Only if we do the action named in some *special* way or circumstances, different from those in which such an act is naturally done (and of course both the normal and the abnormal differ according to what verb in particular is in question) is a modifying expression called for, or even in order. I sit in my chair, in the usual way—I am not in a daze or influenced by threats or the like: here, it will not do to say either that I sat in it intentionally or that I did not sit in it intentionally,[1] nor yet that I sat in it automatically or from habit or what you will. It is bedtime, I am alone, I yawn: but I do not yawn involuntarily (or voluntarily!), nor yet deliberately. To yawn in any such peculiar way is just not to just yawn.

(2) *Limitation of application.*—Expressions modifying verbs, typically adverbs, have limited ranges of application. That is, given any adverb of excuse, such as 'unwittingly' or 'spontaneously' or 'impulsively', it will not be found that it makes good sense to attach it to any and every verb of 'action' in any and every context: indeed, it will often apply only to a comparatively narrow range of such verbs. Something in the lad's upturned face appealed to him, he threw a brick at it—'spontaneously'? The interest then is to discover why some actions can be excused in a particular way but not others, particularly perhaps the latter.[2] This will largely elucidate the meaning of the excuse, and

[1] Caveat or hedge: of course we can say 'I did *not* sit in it "intentionally"' as a way simply of repudiating the suggestion that I sat in it intentionally.

[2] For we are sometimes not so good at observing what we *can't* say as what we can, yet the first is pretty regularly the more revealing.

at the same time will illuminate the characteristics typical of the group of 'actions' it picks out: very often too it will throw light on some detail of the machinery of 'action' in general (see (4)), or on our standards of acceptable conduct (see (5)). It is specially important in the case of some of the terms most favoured by philosophers or jurists to realize that at least in ordinary speech (disregarding back-seepage of jargon) they are not used so universally or so dichotomistically. For example, take 'voluntarily' and 'involuntarily': we may join the army or make a gift voluntarily, we may hiccough or make a small gesture involuntarily, and the more we consider further actions which we might naturally be said to do in either of these ways, the more circumscribed and unlike each other do the two classes become, until we even doubt whether there is *any* verb with which both adverbs are equally in place. Perhaps there are some such; but at least sometimes when we may think we have found one it is an illusion, an apparent exception that really does prove the rule. I can perhaps 'break a cup' voluntarily, *if* that is done, say, as an act of self-impoverishment: and I can perhaps break another involuntarily, *if*, say, I make an involuntary movement which breaks it. Here, plainly, the two acts described each as 'breaking a cup' are really very different, and the one is similar to acts typical of the 'voluntary' class, the other to acts typical of the 'involuntary' class.

(3) *The importance of Negations and Opposites.*—'Voluntarily' and 'involuntarily', then, are not opposed in the obvious sort of way that they are made to be in philosophy or jurisprudence. The 'opposite' or rather 'opposites', of 'voluntarily' might be 'under constraint' of some sort, duress or obligation or influence[1]: the opposite of 'involuntarily' might be 'deliberately' or 'on purpose' or the like. Such divergences in opposites indicate that 'voluntarily' and 'involuntarily', in spite of their apparent connexion, are fish from very different kettles. In general, it will pay us to take nothing for granted or as obvious about negations and opposites. It does not pay to assume that a word must have an opposite, or one opposite, whether it is a 'positive' word like 'wilfully' or a 'negative' word like 'inadvertently'. Rather, we should be asking ourselves such questions as why there is no use for the adverb 'advertently'. For above all it will not do to assume that the 'positive' word must be around to wear the trousers; commonly enough the 'negative' (looking) word marks the (positive) abnormality, while the 'positive' word, *if* it exists, merely

[1]But remember, when I sign a cheque in the normal way, I do *not* do so *either* 'voluntarily' *or* 'under constraint'.

serves to rule out the suggestion of that abnormality. It is natural enough, in view of what was said in (1) above, for the 'positive' word not to be found at all in some cases. I do an act A_1 (say, crush a snail) *inadvertently* if, in the course of executing by means of movements of my bodily parts some other act A_2 (say, in walking down the public path) I fail to exercise such meticulous supervision over the courses of those movements as would have been needed to ensure that they did not bring about the untoward event (here, the impact on the snail).[1] By claiming that A_1 was inadvertent we place it, where we imply it belongs, on this special level, in a class of incidental happenings which must occur in the doing of any physical act. To lift the act out of this class, we need and possess the expression 'not . . . inadvertently': 'advertently', if used for this purpose, would suggest that, if the act was not done inadvertently, then it must have been done noticing what I was doing, which is far from necessarily the case (e.g., if I did it absent-mindedly), or at least that there is *something* in common to the ways of doing all acts not done inadvertently, which is not the case. Again, there is no use for 'advertently' at the *same* level as 'inadvertently': in passing the butter I do not knock over the cream-jug, though I do (inadvertently) knock over the teacup—yet I do not by-pass the cream-jug *advertently*: for at this level, below supervision in detail, *anything* that we do is, if you like, inadvertent, though we only call it so, and indeed only call it something we have done, if there is something untoward about it.

A further point of interest in studying so-called 'negative' terms is the manner of their formation. Why are the words in one group formed with *un-* or *in-*; those in another with *-less* ('aimless', 'reckless', 'heedless', etc.), and those in another with *mis-* ('mistake', 'misconception', 'misjudgement', etc.)? Why care*less*ly but *in*attentively? Perhaps care and attention, so often linked, are rather different. Here are remunerative exercises.

(4) *The machinery of action.*—Not merely do adverbial expressions pick out classes of actions, they also pick out the internal detail of the machinery of doing actions, or the departments into which the

[1] Or analogously: I do an act A_1 (say, divulge my age, or imply you are a liar), *inadvertently* if, in the course of executing by the use of some medium of communication some other act A_2 (say, reminiscing about my war service) I fail to exercise such meticulous supervision over the choice and arrangement of the signs as would have been needed to ensure that. . . . It is interesting to note how such adverbs lead parallel lives, one in connexion with physical actions ('doing') and the other in connexion with acts of communication ('saying'), or sometimes also in connexion with acts of 'thinking' ('inadvertently assumed').

business of doing actions is organized. There is for example the stage at which we have actually to *carry out* some action upon which we embark—perhaps we have to make certain bodily movements or to make a speech. In the course of actually *doing* these things (getting weaving) we have to pay (some) attention to what we are doing and to take (some) care to guard against (likely) dangers: we may need to use judgement or tact: we must exercise sufficient control over our bodily parts: and so on. Inattention, carelessness, errors of judgement, tactlessness, clumsiness, all these and others are ills (with attendant excuses) which affect one specific stage in the machinery of action, the *executive* stage, the stage where we *muff* it. But there are many other departments in the business too, each of which is to be traced and mapped through its cluster of appropriate verbs and adverbs. Obviously there are departments of intelligence and planning, of decision and resolve, and so on: but I shall mention one in particular, too often overlooked, where troubles and excuses abound. It happens to us, in military life, to be in receipt of excellent intelligence, to be also in self-conscious possession of excellent principles (the five golden rules for winning victories), and yet to hit upon a plan of action which leads to disaster. One way in which this can happen is through failure at the stage of *appreciation* of the situation, that is at the stage where we are required to cast our excellent intelligence into such a form, under such heads and with such weights attached, that our equally excellent principles can be brought to bear on it properly, in a way to yield the right answer.[1] So too in real, or rather civilian, life, in moral or practical affairs, we can know the facts and yet look at them mistakenly or perversely, or not fully realize or appreciate something, or even be under a total misconception. Many expressions of excuse indicate failure at this particularly tricky stage: even thoughtlessness, inconsiderateness, lack of imagination, are perhaps less matters of failure in intelligence or planning than might be supposed, and more matters of failure to appreciate the situation. A course of E. M. Forster and we see things differently: yet perhaps we know no more and are no cleverer.

(5) *Standards of the unacceptable.*—It is characteristic of excuses to be 'unacceptable': given, I suppose, almost any excuse, there will be cases of such a kind or of such gravity that 'we will not accept' it. It is interesting to detect the standards and codes we thus invoke.

[1] We know all about how to do quadratics: we know all the needful facts about pipes, cisterns, hours and plumbers: yet we reach the answer '$3\frac{3}{4}$ men'. We have failed to cast our facts correctly into mathematical form.

The extent of the supervision we exercise over the execution of any act can never be quite unlimited, and usually is expected to fall within fairly definite limits ('due care and attention') in the case of acts of some general kind, though of course we set very different limits in different cases. We may plead that we trod on the snail inadvertently: but not on a baby—you ought to look where you're putting your great feet. Of course it *was* (*really*), if you like, inadvertence: but that word constitutes a plea, which isn't going to be allowed, because of standards. And if you try it on, you will be subscribing to such dreadful standards that your last state will be worse than your first. Or again, we set different standards, and will accept different excuses, in the case of acts which are rule-governed, like spelling, and which we are expected absolutely to get right, from those we set and accept for less stereotyped actions: a wrong spelling may be a slip, but hardly an accident, a winged beater may be an accident, but hardly a slip.

(6) *Combination, dissociation and complication.*—A belief in opposites and dichotomies encourages, among other things, a blindness, to the combinations and dissociations of adverbs that are possible, even to such obvious facts as that we can act at once on impulse and intentionally, or that we can do an action intentionally yet for all that not deliberately, still less on purpose. We walk along the cliff, and I feel a sudden impulse to push you over, which I promptly do: I acted on impulse, yet I certainly intended to push you over, and may even have devised a little ruse to achieve it: yet even then I did not act deliberately, for I did not (stop to) ask myself whether to do it or not.

It is worth bearing in mind, too, the general rule that we must not expect to find simple labels for complicated cases. If a mistake results in an accident, it will not do to ask whether 'it' was an accident or a mistake, or to demand some briefer description of 'it'. Here the natural economy of language operates: if the words already available for simple cases suffice in combination to describe a complicated case, there will be need for special reasons before a special new word is invented for the complication. Besides, however well-equipped our language, it can never be forearmed against all possible cases that may arise and call for description: fact is richer than diction.

(7) *Regina v. Finney.*—Often the complexity and difficulty of a case is considerable. I will quote the case of *Regina v. Finney*:[1]
Shrewsbury Assizes. 1874.   12 Cox 625.
Prisoner was indicted for the manslaughter of Thomas Watkins.

[1] A somewhat distressing favourite in the class that Hart used to conduct with me in the years soon after the war. The italics are mine.

The Prisoner was an attendant at a lunatic asylum. Being in charge of a lunatic, who was bathing, he turned on hot water into the bath, and thereby scalded him to death. The facts appeared to be truly set forth in the statement of the prisoner made before the committing magistrate, as follows: 'I had bathed Watkins, and had loosed the bath out. *I intended putting in a clean bath*, and asked Watkins if he would get out. At this time *my attention was drawn* to the next bath by the new attendant, who was asking me a question; and *my attention was taken from the bath* where Watkins was. I put my hand down to turn water on in the bath where Thomas Watkins was. *I did not intend to turn the hot water*, and *I made a mistake in the tap. I did not know what I had done until* I heard Thomas Watkins shout out; and *I did not find my mistake out till* I saw the steam from the water. You cannot get water in this bath when they are drawing water at the other bath; but at other times it shoots out like a water gun when the other baths are not in use. . . . '

(It was proved that the lunatic had such possession of his faculties as would enable him to understand what was said to him, and to get out of the bath.)

A. Young (for Prisoner). The death *resulted from accident*. There was no such *culpable negligence* on the part of the prisoner as will support this indictment. A *culpable mistake*, or some degree of *culpable negligence*, casuing death, will not support a charge of manslaughter; unless the *negligence* be so gross as to be *reckless*. (*R. v. Noakes.*)

Lush, J. To render a person liable for *neglect of duty* there must be such a degree of culpability as to amount to *gross negligence* on his part. If you accept the prisoner's own statement, you find no such amount of *negligence* as would come within this definition. It is not every little *trip or mistake* that will make a man so liable. It was the duty of the attendant not to let hot water into the bath while the patient was therein. According to the prisoner's own account, *he did not believe that* he was letting the hot water in while the deceased remained there. The lunatic was, we have heard, a man capable of getting out by himself and of understanding what was said to him. He was told to get out. A new attendant who had come on this day, was at an adjoining bath and he *took off the prisoner's attention*. Now, if the prisoner, knowing that the man was in the bath, had turned on the tap, and turned on the hot instead of the cold water, I should have said there was gross negligence; for he ought to have looked to see. But from his own account he had told the deceased to get out, and *thought he had got out*. If you think that indicates gross *carelessness*, then you should find the prisoner guilty of manslaughter. But if you think it *inadvertence* not amounting to culpability—i.e., what is properly termed an *accident*—then the prisoner is not liable.

Verdict, Not guilty.

In this case there are two morals that I will point:

(8 ff.) Both counsel and judge make very free use of a large number of terms of excuse, using several as though they were, and even stating them to be, indifferent or equivalent when they are not, and presenting as alternatives those that are not.

(11) It is constantly difficult to be sure *what* act it is that counsel or judge is suggesting might be qualified by what expression of excuse.

The learned judge's concluding direction is a paradigm of these faults.[1] Finney, by contrast, stands out as an evident master of the Queen's English. He is explicit as to each of his acts and states, mental and physical: he uses different, and the correct, adverbs in connexion with each: and he makes no attempt to boil down.

(8) *Small distinctions, and big too.*—It should go without saying that terms of excuse are not equivalent, and that it matters which we use: we need to distinguish inadvertence not merely from (save the mark) such things as mistake and accident, but from such nearer neighbours as, say, aberration and absence of mind. By imagining cases with vividness and fullness we should be able to decide in which precise terms to describe, say, Miss Plimsoll's action in writing, so carefully, 'DAIRY' on her fine new book: we should be able to distinguish between sheer, mere, pure and simple mistake or inadvertence. Yet unfortunately, at least when in the grip of thought, we fail not merely at these stiffer hurdles. We equate even—I have seen it done—'inadvertently' with 'automatically': as though to say I trod on your toe inadvertently means to say I trod on it automatically. Or we collapse succumbing to temptation into losing control of ourselves,—a bad patch, this, for telescoping.[2]

[1] Not but what he probably manages to convey his meaning somehow or other. Judges seem to acquire a knack of conveying meaning, and even carrying conviction, through the use of a pithy Anglo-Saxon which sometimes has literally no meaning at all. Wishing to distinguish the case of shooting at a post in the belief that it was an enemy, *as not* an 'attempt', from the case of picking an empty pocket in the belief that money was in it, which *is* an 'attempt', the judge explains that in shooting at the post 'the man is never on the thing at all'.

[2] Plato, I suppose, and after him Aristotle, fastened this confusion upon us, as bad in its day and way as the later, grotesque, confusion of moral weakness with weakness of will. I am very partial to ice cream, and a bombe is served divided into segments

All this is not so much a *lesson* from the study of excuses as the very object of it.

(9) *The exact phrase and its place in the sentence.*—It is not enough, either, to attend simply to the 'key' word: notice must also be taken of the full and exact form of the expression used. In considering mistakes we have to consider seriatim 'by mistake', 'owing to a mistake', 'mistakenly', 'it was a mistake to', 'to make a mistake in or over or about', 'to be mistaken about', and so on: in considering purpose, we have to consider 'on', 'with the', 'for the', etc., besides 'purposeful', 'purposeless' and the like. These varying expressions may function quite differently—and usually do, or why should we burden ourselves with more than one of them?

Care must be taken too to observe the precise position of an adverbial expression in the sentence. This should of course indicate what verb it is being used to modify: but more than that, the position can also affect the *sense* of the expression, i.e., the way in which

it modifies that verb. Compare, for example:—

   a_1 He clumsily trod on the snail.
   a_2 Clumsily he trod on the snail.
   b_1 He trod clumsily on the snail.
   b_2 He trod on the snail clumsily.

Here, in a_1 and a_2 we describe his treading on the creature at all as a piece of clumsiness, incidental, we imply, to his performance of some other action: but with b_1 and b_2 to tread on it is, very likely, his aim or policy, what we criticize is his execution of the feat.[1] Many adverbs, though far from all (not, e.g., 'purposely') are used in these two typically different ways.

(10) *The style of performance.*—With some adverbs the distinction between the two senses referred to in the last paragraph is carried a stage further. 'He ate his soup deliberately' may mean, like 'He deliberately ate his soup', that his eating his soup was a deliberate act, one perhaps that he thought would annoy somebody, as it would corresponding one to one with the persons at High Table: I am tempted to help myself to two segments and do so, thus succumbing to temptation and even conceivably (but why necessarily?) going against my principles. But do I lose control of myself? Do I raven, do I snatch the morsels from the dish and wolf them down, impervious to the consternation of my colleagues? Not a bit of it. We often succumb to temptation with calm and even with finesse.

[1] As a matter of fact, most of these examples *can* be understood the other way, especially if we allow ourselves inflexions of the voice, or commas, or contexts. a_2 might be a poetic inversion for b_2: b_1, perhaps with commas round the 'clumsily', might be used for a_1: and so on. Still, the two senses are clearly enough distinguishable.

more commonly if he deliberately ate *my* soup, and which he decided
to do: but it will often mean that he went through the performance of
eating his soup in a noteworthy manner or *style*—pause after each
mouthful, careful choice of point of entry for the spoon, sucking of
moustaches, and so on. That is, it will mean that he ate *with* deliberation rather than *after* deliberation. The style of the performance,
slow and unhurried, is understandably called 'deliberate' because
each movement *has the typical look* of a deliberate act: but it is
scarcely being said that the making of each motion *is* a deliberate act or
that he is 'literally' deliberating. This case, then, is more extreme than
that of 'clumsily', which does in both uses describe literally a manner
of performing.

It is worth watching out for this secondary use when scrutinizing
any particular adverbial expression: when it definitely does not exist,
the reason is worth inquiring into. Sometimes it is very hard to be
sure whether it does exist or does not: it does, one would think, with
'carelessly', it does not with 'inadvertently', but does it or does it not
with 'absent-mindedly' or 'aimlessly'? In some cases a word akin to
but distinct from the primary adverb is used for this special role of
describing a style of performance: we use 'purposefully' in this way,
but never 'purposely'.

(11) *What modifies what?* The Judge in *Regina* v. *Finney* does not make
clear what event is being excused in what way. 'If you think that
indicates gross carelessness, then . . . But if you think it inadvertence
not amounting to culpability—i.e., what is properly called an
accident—then . . . ' Apparently he means that Finney may have
turned on the hot tap inadvertently[1]: does he mean also that the tap
may have been turned accidentally, or rather that *Watkins may have been
scalded* and killed accidentally? And was the carelessness in turning
the tap or in thinking Watkins had got out? Many disputes as to what
excuse we should properly use arise because we will not trouble to state
explicitly *what* is being excused.

To do so is all the more vital because it is in principle always open

---

[1]What Finney says is different: he says he 'made a mistake in the tap'. This is
the basic use of 'mistake', where we simply, and not necessarily accountably, take the
wrong one. Finney here attempts to account for his mistake, by saying that his
attention was distracted. But suppose the order is 'Right turn' and I turn left: no
doubt the sergeant will insinuate that my attention was distracted, or that I cannot
distinguish my right from my left—but it wasn't and I can, this was a simple, pure
mistake. As often happens. Neither I nor the sergeant will suggest that there was any
accident, or any inadvertence either. If Finney had turned the hot tap inadvertently, then
it would have been knocked, say, in reaching for the cold tap: a different story.

to us, along various lines, to describe or refer to 'what I did' in so
many different ways. This is altogether too large a theme to elaborate
here. Apart from the more general and obvious problems of the use of
'tendentious' descriptive terms, there are many special problems in
the particular case of 'actions'. Should we say, are we saying, that he
took her money, or that he robbed her? That he knocked a ball into a
hole, or that he sank a putt? That he said 'Done', or that he accepted
an offer? How far, that is, are motives, intentions and conventions to
be part of the description of actions? And more especially here, what
is *an* or *one* or *the* action? For we can generally split up what might
be named as one action in several distinct ways, into different *stretches*
or *phases* or *stages*. Stages have already been mentioned: we can dis-
mantle the machinery of the act, and describe (and excuse) separately
the intelligence, the appreciation, the planning, the decision, the
execution and so forth. Phases are rather different: we can say that he
painted a picture or fought a campaign, or else we can say that first he
laid on this stroke of paint and then that, first he fought this action and
then that. Stretches are different again: a single term descriptive of
what he did may be made to cover either a smaller or a larger stretch of
events, those excluded by the narrower description being then called
'consequences' or 'results' or 'effects' or the like of his act. So here
we can describe Finney's act *either* as turning on the hot tap, which he
did by mistake, with the result that Watkins was scalded, *or* as
scalding Watkins, which he did *not* do by mistake.

It is very evident that the problems of excuses and those of the
different descriptions of actions are throughout bound up with each
other.

(12). *Trailing clouds of etymology*.—It is these considerations that
bring us up so forcibly against some of the most difficult words in the
whole story of Excuses, such words as 'result', 'effect' and 'consequence', or again as 'intention', 'purpose' and 'motive'. I will
mention two points of method which are, experience has convinced
me, indispensable aids at these levels.

One is that a word never—well, hardly ever—shakes off its etymology and its formation. In spite of all changes in and extensions
of and additions to its meanings, and indeed rather pervading and
governing these, there will still persist the old idea. In an *accident* something befalls: by *mistake* you take the wrong one: in *error* you stray:
when you act *deliberately* you act after weighing it up (*not* after
thinking out ways and means). It is worth asking ourselves whether
we know the etymology of 'result' or of 'spontaneously', and worth

remembering that 'unwillingly' and 'involuntarily' come from very different sources.

And the second point is connected with this. Going back into the history of a word, very often into Latin, we come back pretty commonly to pictures or *models* of how things happen or are done. These models may be fairly sophisticated and recent, as is perhaps the case with 'motive' or 'impulse', but one of the commonest and most primitive types of model is one which is apt to baffle us through its very naturalness and simplicity. We take *some very simple action*, like shoving a stone, usually as done by and viewed by oneself, and use *this*, with the features distinguishable in it, as our model in terms of which to talk about other actions and events: and we continue to do so, scarcely realizing it, even when these other actions are pretty remote and perhaps much more interesting to us in their own right than the acts originally used in constructing the model ever were, and even when the model is really distorting the facts rather than helping us to observe them. In primitive cases we may get to see clearly the differences between, say, 'results', 'effects' and 'consequences', and yet discover that these differences are no longer clear, and the terms themselves no longer of real service to us, in the more complicated cases where we had been bandying them about most freely. A model must be recognized for what it is. 'Causing', I suppose, was a notion taken from a man's own experience of doing simple actions, and by primitive man every event was construed in terms of this model: every event has a cause, that is, every event is an action done by somebody— if not by a man, then by a quasi-man, a spirit. When, later, events which are *not* actions are realized to be such, we still say that they must be 'caused', and the word snares us: we are struggling to ascribe to it a new, unanthropomorphic meaning, yet constantly, in searching for its analysis, we unearth and incorporate the lineaments of the ancient model. As happened even to Hume, and consequently to Kant. Examining such a word historically, we may well find that it has been extended to cases that have by now too tenuous a relation to the model case, that it is a source of confusion and superstition.

There is too another danger in words that invoke models, half-forgotten or not. It must be remembered that there is no necessity whatsoever that the various models used in creating our vocabulary, primitive or recent, should all fit together neatly as parts into one single, total model or scheme of, for instance, the doing of actions. It is possible, and indeed highly likely, that our assortment of models will include some, or many, that are overlapping, conflicting, or more generally simply *disparate*.[1]

(13) In spite of the wide and acute observation of the phenomena of action embodied in ordinary speech, modern scientists have been able, it seems to me, to reveal its inadequacy at numerous points, if only because they have had access to more comprehensive data and have studied them with more catholic and dispassionate interest than the ordinary man, or even the lawyer, has had occasion to do. I will conclude with two examples.

Observation of animal behaviour shows that regularly, when an animal is embarked on some recognizable pattern of behaviour but meets in the course of it with an insuperable obstacle, it will betake itself to energetic, but quite unrelated, activity of some wild kind such as standing on its head. This phenomenon is called 'displacement behaviour' and is well identifiable. If now, in the light of this, we look back at ordinary human life, we see that displacement behaviour bulks quite large in it: yet we have apparently no word, or at least no clear and simple word, for it. If, when thwarted, we stand on our heads or wiggle our toes, then we aren't exactly *just* standing on our heads, don't you know, in the ordinary way, yet is there any convenient adverbial expression we can insert to do the trick? 'In desperation'?

Take, again, 'compulsive' behaviour, however exactly psychologists define it, compulsive washing for example. There are of course hints in ordinary speech that we do things in this way—'just feel I have to', 'shouldn't feel comfortable unless I did', and the like: but there is no adverbial expression satisfactorily pre-empted for it, as 'compulsively' is. This is understandable enough, since compulsive behaviour, like displacement behaviour, is not in general going to be of great practical importance.

Here I leave and commend the subject to you.

[1]This is by way of a general warning in philosophy. It seems to be too readily assumed that if we can only discover the true meanings of each of a cluster of key terms, usually historic terms, that we use in some particular field (as, for example, 'right', 'good' and the rest in morals), then it must without question transpire that each will fit into place in some single, interlocking, consistent, conceptual scheme. Not only is there no reason to assume this, but all historical probability is against it, especially in the case of a language derived from such various civilizations as ours is. We may cheerfully use, and with weight, terms which are not so much head-on incompatible as simply disparate, which just don't fit in or even on. Just as we cheerfully subscribe to, or have the grace to be torn between, simply disparate ideals—why *must* there be a conceivable amalgam, the Good Life for Man?

II

BASIC ACTIONS

Arthur C. Danto

'Well, why should we want to know?' said Verity, giving a yawn or
causing herself to give one.

    I. Compton-Burnett, *Two Worlds and Their Ways*

I

'The man M causes the stone S to move.' This is a very general description of a very familiar sort of episode. It is so general, indeed,
that it does not tell us whether or not M has performed an action. The
description holds in either case; so it could have been an action.
Without pausing to inquire what further features are required for it
definitely to have been an action, let us merely note that *there are*
actions that fall under the general description of 'causing something
to happen'. Yet, since this description leaves it unclear whether or
not an action has been performed, performing an action cannot be
one of the truth conditions for 'causing something to happen'. And
since this description cuts across those two cases, we may assume we
are employing the same sense of the expression 'causes something to
happen' in both. Presumably, we are using 'causes' in just the same
sense whether we say that the man M causes the stone S to move *or* we
say that the stone S causes the pebble P to move. If it *is* clear from
the latter sentence that an action has *not* been performed, this clarity
will be due to certain facts about stones rather than to any difference
in the concept of causality. It is commonly assumed that stones never
perform actions, although men sometimes do. Hence the indefinite-
ness of our original sentence is not due to any ambiguity in the concept
of causality, but rather to certain facts about men, or to certain
assumed facts. The concept of causality allows us to ignore differences
between men and stones, as well as differences between performing an
action and not.

    I shall persist in speaking of *individuals* (the man M, the stone S)

From *American Philosophical Quarterly*, 2 (1965), pp. 141–8. Reprinted by permission
of the author and the *American Philosophical Quarterly*.

causing things to happen, even though our concept of causality has been classically analyzed as a relationship between pairs of *events*. According to the classical analysis, the movement of the pebble *P* is one event, the effect of another event, which I shall, with studied ambiguity, simply designate an *S*-event, in this case its cause. Comparably, the movement of *S* in my other example is one event, the effect of another event, similarly and no less ambiguously to be designated an *M*-event, which is its cause. And this *M*-event, whether or not it is an action performed by *M*, is correctly (if rather generally) to be described as *causing something to happen*—namely, the movement of *S*.

I shall now suppose that my original sentence in fact describes an action performed by *M* (moving the stone *S*). Of this particular spatial translation of *S* we may say three distinct and relevant things: that it is (*a*) an action, performed by *M*; that it is (*b*) something that was *caused* to happen (in this case by *M*); and that it is (*c*) the effect of an event distinct from itself (in this case the *M*-event). That this event can be both (*a*) and (*b*) follows from the remarks in the first paragraph. That—disregarding the special information in parentheses—(*c*) must hold if (*b*) does—follows from the analysis of causality referred to in the second paragraph. That it is (*b*) follows, I suppose, from the fact that *S* is a stone: stones don't *just* start to move without something causing them to move.

We must now look into the *M*-event itself. Do all three characterizations apply to *it*? This, I fear, cannot be decided without investigation. Let us suppose, however, that the *M*-event is both (*a*) and (*b*), for it might well be. Then it must also be (*c*), and there must then be yet another event, distinct from it, which is its cause. This may be yet a further *M*-event, and about it we may raise the same question. It would be rash to claim that we have slid into an infinite regress, damaging or otherwise. But if a given *M*-event is both (*a*) and (*b*) and, hence, (*c*), then ultimately its being (*c*) must lead us to a further *M*-event, which is (*a*) and *not* (*b*). And unless some *M*-events are (*a*) and not (*b*), *no* *M*-events are ever (*a*). That is, if there are any actions at all, there must be two distinct *kinds* of actions: those performed by an individual *M*, which he may be said to have *caused* to happen; and those actions, also performed by *M*, which he cannot be said to have caused to happen. The latter I shall designate as *basic actions*.

In this paper, I shall defend (and explore the consequences of) four theses which I regard as fundamental to the theory of action:

(1) If there are any actions at all, there are basic actions.

(2) There are basic actions.

(3) Not every action is a basic action.[1]

(4) If *a* is an action performed by *M*, then either *a* is a basic action of *M*, or else it is the effect of a chain of causes the originating member of which is a basic action of *M*.

I wish first to make quite clear the sense in which an individual does not cause his basic actions to happen. When an individual *M* performs a basic action *a*, there is no event distinct from *a* that both stands to *a* as cause to effect *and* is an action performed by *M*. So when *M* performs a basic action, he does nothing first that causes it to happen. It will be convenient to consider two possible objections to this.

It may be objected, first, that there are or may be other senses of 'causes' than the sense mentioned above, in accordance with which it would be proper to say that *M* causes his basic actions to happen. Thus, *if* raising an arm were an instance of a basic action, an individual who does this might still be said to cause it to happen in some sense of 'cause' other than the sense that I reject in application to basic actions. I accept this objection: there *may be* such other senses of 'cause'. But (i) we should still require exactly the same distinction that I am urging within the class of actions, and I should therefore be defending the *verbally* distinct thesis that unless there were actions an individual causes to happen in this *new* sense, there would be no actions he caused to happen in the original sense, either. So, unless there were actions of the former sort, causing a stone to move would, for example, never be an *action* that anyone performed (although men might still cause stones to move, since performing an action is not a truth-condition for 'causing something to happen'). And (ii) this new sense of 'cause' would *not* apply *whether or not* an action had been performed. It should, indeed, be absolutely clear from the sentence 'M caused *a* to happen'—using this special sense of 'cause'—that *M had* performed an action. Those who find it convenient to maintain that the concept of causality is invariant to the distinction between performing an action and not, would have as little use for this new sense of 'cause' as I do. Neither they nor I would want to say that *stones* cause *anything* to happen in this new sense of 'cause'. Not that I wish to restrict the performance of basic actions to

---

[1]Thesis (3) is explored in detail in my paper, 'What We Can Do', *The Journal of Philosophy*, vol. 60 (July, 1963), pp. 435–45.

men alone. Other individuals may, for all I know, perform them as well. Some theologians have spoken as though everything done by God were a basic action. This would prohibit us, of course, from saying that God caused anything to happen (the making of the Universe would be a basic action.) And, for reasons which will soon emerge, this would make the ways of God inscrutable indeed.

It may be objected, second, that if we take the absence of a cause to be the distinguishing mark of a basic action, then we must class as basic actions a great many events that we should be disinclined, on other grounds, to accept as actions at all, e.g., the uniform rectilinear motion of an isolated particle, or perhaps any instance of radioactive decay. This objection is readily deflected. I have not claimed that basic actions are not caused, but only that a man performing one does not cause it by performing some other action that stands to it as cause to effect. Moreover, the absence of a cause would not be a sufficient criterion for a basic action, even if basic actions *were* uncaused. It would serve only to mark off a special class of actions from the rest. Of course, only what is already an action can be a *basic* action. And I have not so much as tried to say what are the general criteria for actions.

II

I have avoided citing unconditional instances of basic actions, in part because any expression I might use, e.g., 'moving a limb,' could also be used to designate something that was caused to happen, or something that was not an action, much less a basic one. I think there is nothing that is always and in each of its instances an un-mistakably basic action. This is reflected by language in the fact that from the bare description 'M's limb moved', for example, one could not tell whether M had performed a basic action or even an action. Nor could one tell this by observing only the motion of the limb without bringing in differentiating contextual features. I have accordingly contented myself with the neutral expression 'M-event', declaring it to be a basic action when I required an instance.

Now I wish to specify some of the differentiating contextual features, and I shall consider four distinct cases, all of which might indifferently be covered by the same description, so that the descrip-tion alone leaves it unclear whether an action has been performed or not. Of the four cases, three (C-1, C-2, C-4) will indeed be actions, and of these one (*C-4*) will be a basic action. The four cases together might be termed a *declaration* of the description. Not every such description admits of the full declension, for some appear never to be exemplified as basic actions at all. 'Moving a stone', I should think, never, or not ordinarily, is exemplified as a basic action, though we have seen that it may be exemplified by an action. I want to begin with a deliberately controversial example and shall decline the expression '*M* laughs'.

C-1. *M causes himself to laugh*. I am thinking here of cases where someone does something to make himself laugh, and does not simply laugh because of something he happens to do. Thus I may do something ridiculous and laugh because I find it so, but I did not do this ridiculous thing in order to make myself laugh. Again, I sniff a cartridge of nitrous oxide, not knowing it to be nitrous oxide, but just to find out what it is. But, since it is nitrous oxide, I laugh, though I did not sniff to make myself laugh. I wish to include only cases where I do something ridiculous or sniff from a private cartridge of nitrous oxide *in order to* laugh, perhaps because I think laughter good for the liver or because I just enjoy laughing and cannot always wait for someone or something to come along and cause me to laugh. I definitely want to exclude a comedian who laughs at some reruns of his antic films (unless he had them rerun for this special purpose), and definitely want to include someone who deliberately engages in auto-titillation to excite spasmodic laughter. Doubtless, episodes falling under *C-1* are rare in normal adults in our culture, but this is irrelevant. Also irrelevant is the fact that people don't laugh *at* the nitrous oxide they sniff, though they do laugh at the silly faces they pull, for their own delectation, in mirrors.

C-2. *Someone or something other than M causes M to laugh*. This is the typical case for adults and children in our culture. It is for my purposes again irrelevant whether the cause of *M*'s laughter is also its object, or whether it has an object at all (as it does not if he is tickled or submitted to nitrous oxide). Similarly, it is irrelevant whether, in case someone causes *M* to laugh, the former has performed an action or not, whether, that is, he did what he did in order to make *M* laugh. For it is what *M* does that uniquely concerns us here.

C-3. *M suffers a nervous disorder symptomized by spasmodic laughter*. This is comparable, say, to a tic: *M* laughs unpredictably, and for 'no reason'. Such laughter is mirthless, of course, but so are some instances falling under the two first cases. It may be argued that the entire case falls under *C-2*, and that in identifying it as the symptom of a nervous disorder, I have marked off a class of causes for M's laughter. Still, the case requires special consideration, in that M's laughing here is never an action, whereas his laughter under C-2 sometimes *is*.

C-4. M has the true power of laughing. By this I mean that M laughs when he wants to without (in contrast with C-1) having to cause himself to laugh; without (in contrast with C-2) someone or something having to cause him to laugh; without, finally, as in C-3, suffering from the relevant nervous disorder. This does not mean that M is normal, but only that his abnormality is of a benign sort; i.e., it is by way of a gift. His laughing may have an object: he may, when he wishes, direct a stream of laughter at whom or what he chooses, without the chosen object ever being a *cause* of his laughing.

Instances falling under C-4 are perhaps rare, but these alone would qualify as basic actions performed by M when 'M laughs' is true. I have identified the case not so much by specifying what differentiating contextual features must be present, but by specifying what differentiating contextual features must be *absent*. Notice that M's laughing here differs markedly from the ability most of us have of making laugh-like noises, e.g., for the sake of politeness, or to save our reputation for seeing a joke when we don't see it, or to play a mocker's role in an amateur theatrical. Most of us can pretend so to laugh: but I speak here of laughing, not of 'laughing'.

I want now to comment on these four cases.

When M laughs under C-1, we may say of his laughing three distinct things: that it is (*a*) an action of M's; that it is (*b*) something that M causes to happen; and that it is (*c*) the effect of some event, distinct from itself (an M-event) which is its cause. M's laughing here is an action in just the same sense in which his causing a stone to move is an action. Causing himself to laugh is the action he performed, though of course the description 'M caused himself to laugh' leaves it unclear, as in the case of the stone, whether he performed an action at all. One could mark that difference only by bringing in the general differentiating features of action.

In C-2, M does not cause himself to laugh, and one may find reasons for balking at the claim that his laughing, in such a case, is an action of his at all. For consider this argument. When M causes a stone S to move, we may agree that the action is M's. But we reject the claim that it is an action of S's. So parity suggests that when someone moves M to laughter, this may be an action performed by the former, but not an action of M's.

What I must do is to show that parity is inoperative, and so justify my claim that instances of *C-2* are actions in contrast with instances of *C-3*. Well, I shall somewhat artificially suggest that *M*'s action here requires this description: what he does is to *not not* laugh. The double negative is not, in the language of action, a triviality. Logically, of course, the double negative of a proposition is just that proposition, and from a strictly logical point of view, we could say the same thing, albeit more awkwardly, with 'The man *M* causes the stone *S* to not not move' as we straightforwardly say with 'The man *M* caused the stone *S* to move'. I wish, in fact, to retain that regular inferential feature of double negation which allows us to proceed from not not *A* to *A*, but for the case of action I wish to exclude the reverse inference. For my double negative marks the case of *negligence*, and whether a negligence is to be ascribed to someone is a case for independent investigation. So, pending such investigation, we cannot say, on the basis of knowing that a man laughs, that he is to be charged with negligence. And for this reason we cannot automatically go from 'laughs' to 'not not laughs.' Indeed, since we don't ascribe negligence to stones, it would be invalid, given my convention, to proceed from 'the stone moves' to 'the stone not not moves'.

Do we quite want to say, then, that *C-2* is to be restated thus: *Someone or something other than M causes M to not not laugh?* Perhaps we would, in spite of flaunting usage. What we would be saying, however, is only this: that *M* was excited to laugh and did nothing to inhibit his laughter. And it is our common assumption that men are normally capable of doing something which, in effect, stops the flow of laughter from issuing forth in, say, public guffaws. Whether men are called upon to exercise these inhibitory practices varies from context to context: in the music hall there is licence to suspend them, to 'let oneself go', but at High Mass there is not. It is in such contexts only that laughter is *pronounced* a negligence, but blaming, surely, does not make of something an action when it would not otherwise have been so. It is only insofar as something is an action already that blaming it, or blaming someone for doing it, is appropriate.

With regard to *C-3*, however, the laughter stands liable to no special charge of negligence: his laughing fails to be a case of not not laughing, for identification of it as a nervous disorder, or in the syndrome of one, locates it beyond the control of the man who is so afflicted. It is, indeed, almost a paradigm case of this: like a hiccough. One *might* blame the man for being in a place where his symptom, easily mistakable as a negligence, might break out unpredictably. Or we might blame him again for a kind of negligence in 'not doing something about it', viz., going to a nerve specialist, assuming there is a known cure. At all events, it is plain enough why C-3 differs from C-2. The critical issue, of course, is the matter of *control*, and this brings us to C-4. And the rest of this paper is by way of a comment on C-4.

Most readers, I think, will resist the suggestion that C-4 is a case of action. There is good reason for this. For most of us, laughing as a *basic action* is unintelligible. I shall hope to show why this is so, and showing it will involve a demonstration of thesis (2). Meanwhile, the reader might ponder the precise analogue to this in the case of *moving an arm*, which admits of a full declension. Thus C-1: M causes his arm to move, i.e., by striking it with his other arm; C-2: someone or something other than M causes M's arm to move, e.g., by striking it; C-3: M suffers from a nervous disorder, so his arm moves spasmodically and unpredictably, as a kind of tic; and C-4: M moves his arm without suffering from a nervous disorder, without someone or something causing it to move, without having to do anything to cause it to move. Here, I am certain, C-4 is the *typical* case. Moving an arm is one of the standard basic actions. If we now seek to determine in what way this behaviour *is* intelligible, we should have no great difficulty in seeing why laughing under C-4 is *not*.

III

Suppose now that moving a stone is an action performed by M. It is difficult to suppose that *moving a stone* admits of a full declension, largely because it seems to lack cases for C-3 and C-4. In fact there are difficulties in finding instances for C-1 and C-2 unless we change the sense of possession (M's arm, M's stone) from philosophical to legal ownership. But for the moment I shall be concerned only with the fact that we move stones only by causing them to move. This then means that, in order to cause the motion of the stone, something else must be done, or must happen, which is an event distinct from the motion of the stone, and which stands to it as cause to effect. Now this other event may or may not be a basic action of M's. But if it is not, and if it remains nevertheless true that moving the stone *is* an action of his, then there must be something else that M does, which causes something to happen which in turn causes the motion of the stone. And *this* may be a basic action or it may not. But now this goes on forever unless, at some point, a basic action is performed by *M*. For suppose every action were a case of the agent causing something to happen. This means, each time he does *a*, he must independently do *b*, which causes *a* to happen. But then, in order to do *b*, he must first independently do *c*, which causes *b* to happen. . . . This quickly entails that the agent could perform no action at all. If, accordingly, there are any actions at all of the sort described by 'causing something to happen', there must be actions which are *not* caused to happen by the man who performs them. And these are basic actions.

But this argument is perfectly general. If there are any actions at all, there are basic actions. This is a proof of thesis (1). Moreover, if *M* performs an action describable by 'causing something to happen', he must also, as part of what he does, peform an action that he does not cause to happen. And this is a proof of thesis (4). It would be a proof of thesis (2) if in fact there were actions described as 'causing something to happen'. This would then require us to accept thesis (3) as true: for such an action would not be a basic action, and so not every action is basic.

I do not wish to suggest, however, that the only proof we are entitled to, for the existence of basic actions, is by way of a transcendental deduction, for I believe we all know, in a direct and intuitive way, that there are basic actions, and which actions are basic ones. To show that we do know this will clarify one of the ways in which laughing is a controversial instance of a basic action.

I must make a few preliminary remarks. First, every *normal person* has just the same *repertoire R* of basic actions, and having *R* is what defines a normal person for the theory of action. Second, persons may be *positively abnormal* when their repertoire of basic actions includes actions not included in *R*, and may be *negatively abnormal* when actions included in *R* are not included in their repertoire. Some persons may be both positively and negatively abnormal, e.g., someone who laughs as a basic action but who is paralysed in one arm. If someone's repertoire is empty, he is capable of no basic actions, and hence of no actions. Such a deprived entity is a *pure patient*, e.g., like a stone. Plainly, our repertoire of actions is greater than our repertoire of basic actions, though a being who performed every possible action and all of whose actions were basic actions may be conceived of: such a being would be a *pure agent*. For the present, however, I am concerned with beings intermediate between pure patients and pure agents, and I want now to say that basic actions are *given* to such beings in two distinct senses, each of which bears a definite analogy to a sense that the term has in the theory of knowledge.[1]

(i) In the theory of knowledge, to say that p is *given* is in part to point a contrast: one is saying that p is not inferred from some other proposition. Analogously, when I speak of an action as given, I shall mean to say, in effect, that it is a basic action, and point a contrast with actions we *cause* to happen. The notion of givenness is understood this way: p is a starting point for an inference to another and (commonly) different proposition q for which p provides at least part of the evidence. Analogously, an action a, if a basic action, is a starting point for the performance of another action b, of which it is at least part of the cause. 'Is caused by' and 'is inferred from' are analogous relations in the theories of knowledge and of action, respectively.

(ii) It has been argued that the distinction between *basic sentences* and sentences of other kinds is not ultimate, that a sentence which, in one context, is indeed a starting point for an inference to another, may, in a different context, itself be inferred to, and hence an end point in an inference.[2] Analogously, an action a may, in one context, be a starting point and basic, while it may be caused to happen in a different one. There is some justice in this latter claim: as we have seen, one cannot tell from the bare description 'moving an arm' whether a basic action is referred to, or even an action. But, thinking now of sentences, perhaps some restriction can be put on the *kind* of sentence which can be given in sense (i). If p is given in one context and inferred in another, there might nevertheless be sentences which are never

---

[1]The analogy between theory of knowledge and theory of action runs very deep indeed, almost as though they were isomorphic models for some calculus. Obviously, there are things we can say about actions that do not hold for cognitions, etc., but this means very little. Suppose we have two models M-i and M-j for a calculus C, and suppose that 'star' plays in the same role in M-i that 'book' plays in M-j. It is hardly an argument against their both being models for C that we don't print stars or that books are not centres of solar systems. I shall use theory-of-knowledge features as a guide for structuring the theory of action. When the analogy gives way, it will be interesting to see why it does.

[2]Though not always without some awkwardness. Suppose it were held that only sentences can be given which have the form of first-person reports of sense-experience, e.g., 'I now see a reddish x . . .' Such a sentence is not easily rendered as the conclusion of an inference, though it can be so rendered, I suppose, if I both knew that something x had an unmistakable taste and that whatever has this taste is red. Then, by tasting x and seeing only its silhouette, I might feel secure in inferring that I was seeing a reddish x. Of course there are philosophically crucial senses of 'see' which would rule this out, and make it, indeed, self-contradictory to say both 'I see a reddish x' and 'I see the black silhouette of x'.

basic and always are inferred. And a corresponding restriction might hold in the theory of action: even if any action that is ever basic might, under a sufficiently general description, be caused to happen in another context, there might be actions that never are basic under any description. In the theory of knowledge, one such restriction is often defended, namely that basic sentences are those and only those which can be conclusively verified by sense experience, and that no other kind of sentence ever can be given. But within the class of potentially given sentences, a division might be made along the customary lines of sense-modality, i. e., those verified by seeing, or by audition, or by touch, etc. We might then define an *epistemically* normal person as one who experiences in all modes. A negatively abnormal person would then be deficient in at least one such mode, e.g., is blind; and a positively abnormal person then experiences in some mode outside the normal repertoire, e.g., has some 'sixth sense'. The analogy to the theory of action is obvious. But by means of it we may introduce our second sense of given: the normal modes of experience are 'given' in the sense that they constitute the standard cognitive equipment. The normal person has various classes of starting points for inferences as he has various classes of starting points for actions. These are given in the sense that they are not for the most part *acquired*. Thus we speak of the 'gift of sight,' etc. This does not mean that there need be any sentences in the super-structure to which a negatively abnormal person might not infer: he is deficient only at the base: and then not *totally* deficient (or if he is, then he cannot have any empirical knowledge, is *cognitively impotent*). And similarly, *toutes proportions gardées*, with the negatively abnormal person as defined in the theory of action.

Now when a blind man says that he can know whether a certain object is red or not, there are two senses or uses of 'can' that are compatible with his abnormality. He must mean either that he can *infer* to '*x* is red' from other sentences or that his case is not medically hopeless, that by means of a cure he may be restored to that state of normality in which such sentences may be known by him directly and not, as it were, *merely* by means of inference. Yet there is a true and in fact an *analytic* sense in which a blind man cannot know whether a certain object is red, nor, on certain accounts of meaning, so much as know what such a sentence *means* (the non-analytic senses are usually false). The situation of a *paralysed* man is perfectly analogous. When he sincerely says that he can move his arm, he must mean either that he can *cause* it to move, or that his situation is not medically hopeless. But, in again a true and an analytical sense, he cannot move his arm and does not know, does not so much as understand, what it means to move his arm in the way in which a normal person understands this. For this is the kind of understanding that is alone given to those who have the power to move their arms in the normal, basic way. This kind of understanding cannot so much as be conveyed to a negatively abnormal person while he is so.

Some of the chief difficulties philosophers have encountered in the theory of action are due to their having approached it from the point of view of the negatively abnormal. From *that* point of view, basic action is hopelessly mysterious. There is, however, perhaps no better way of eliciting the quality of our knowledge of these things than to think of endeavouring to remove the mysteriousness surrounding these actions in the thwarted comprehension of the negatively abnormal person. We may achieve some sympathy for his plight by imagining *ourselves* similarly confronting someone who is *positively* abnormal, who can perform, as a basic action, what we at best can cause to happen, and then asking *him* to give us an understanding of his gift. The fact is that we cannot explain to the negatively abnormal, nor can the positively abnormal person explain to us, the way in which the basic action is performed (and this must be appreciated in the same way as the impossibility of explaining to a blind man what red literally looks like, or, if you wish, of our understanding what ultra-violet literally looks like). Suppose—just to take one case—a paralytic asks us what we do *first* when we raise an arm. We should be obliged to say we cannot answer, not because we do not know or understand what we do, but because we know and understand that there is *nothing* we do first. There is no series of steps we must run through, and since the request is implicitly for a *recipe*, we cannot say how we move our arm. A basic action is perfectly simple in the same sense in which the old 'simple ideas' were said to be: they were not compounded out of anything more elementary than themselves, but were instead the ultimately simple elements out of which other ideas were compounded.

In one sense, then, we do, and in another we do not, know how we move an arm. But the sense in which we do not know is inappropriate. It is that sense which requires an *account*, and our incapacity for giving any such account is what has induced puzzlement, among philosophers and others, concerning the moving of an arm (and other basic acts generally). But this puzzlement should be dissipated upon the recognition that we have made a grammatical mistake in the inflected language of action. We have taken 'moving an arm' as always a case of C-1, when *in fact C-4* is the standard case for normal persons moving normal arms normally. But having once committed this mistake, we look for a cause that is not there. And failing to find what we ought never to have expected to find, we complain that we do not know how we do move our arms. But of course we know. It is only that we cannot explain the manner of its doing. For there is no action, distinct from the action itself, to be put into the *explanans*. This is due to what I am terming the *givenness* of basic actions. Reference to basic actions belongs in the explanantia for explaining how things are done. So the paralytic, as long as he remains one, cannot understand: *Just raising the arm is what we do first.*

IV

A paralytic might think there is some *effort* he is not putting forth, by which, if he did or could put it forth, he might as a consequence move his arm. But I want to say that he cannot try to move his arm if moving his arm is not already in his repertoire of basic actons. So in a sense he is right. If he could make the required effort, he could move his arm. But he cannot make that effort, cannot try, for he cannot in the only appropriate sense move his arm.

Consider the analogous situation with someone epistemically abnormal, say a deaf man. To ask a deaf man to try to hear a certain sound is rendered inappropriate by the fact that he is deaf. To try to hear, say, faint and distant music is to make an effortful listening. Only those who can already hear can make this effort. And what would count as trying (listening) in the deaf man's case? He could cup his ear, could place his ear to the ground, could contort his face and close his eyes. All this, however, is the pantomime of listening. Had he grinned or wagged a finger, it would have been as helpful. For there is no one thing that is better than any other in his situation. It is exactly this way with trying to move an arm. It is appropriate only to ask someone to try to move his arm when something externally inhibits normal movement, e.g. the arms are pinioned, and cannot be moved *freely* and *without effort*. But the paralytic cannot move his arm at all.

Consider these cases:

(*a*) I am a normal person who has swallowed a drug which gradually takes away the power to move an arm, rendering me, so long as it is in full effect, negatively abnormal. I make tests at five-minute intervals. It gets harder and harder to move my arm. And then I reach a point where I cannot move my arm and cannot *try* to. I have lost the power of trying, together with the power for doing.

(*b*) Someone thinks it would be spectacular to be able to extend and retract his fingernails, the way a cat does with its claws. We tell him it cannot be done, and he retorts that no one has ever tried, and he means to try. But in what should his trying consist? He could shake his fingers hard, could order them to extend, could pray, or could draw his soul up into a vast single wish. There is no rational way, for there is no way at all for a normal person. I don't mean that no one is or ever will be able to move his nails and to try to move them (e.g. with tight gloves on). If a man were prepared to suffer some sort of surgery, he might be able to cause his nails to go in and out, but we had not understood that he meant this by 'trying'. It is after all not the way cats do it. It is more the way we move a loose tooth.

(*c*) I am a normal person, challenged to move a normal stone. I take the challenge to imply the stone is not normal—perhaps it has some incredible density, or is fixed to a shaft driven deeply into the earth. But I decide to try, and the stone moves quite easily, having been a normal stone all along. So I conclude that the challenge was not normal. It turns out I was being asked to move the stone 'the way I move my arm'. But this is not something I even can try to do. I can, with ridiculous ease, cause the stone to move. So I can try to cause it to move as well. But I cannot try to move it as a basic action—that would be a proper encounter with nothingness.

One can do with effort only what one can do effortlessly; and 'trying', the effort of will, is not something apart from the action that stands to it as cause to effect. It is the required action already being performed in untoward circumstances. Doing something with effort is not doing two things, any more than doing something gracefully is doing two things. Moving an arm is not then the result of an act of will: it *is* an act of will. But to speak of an act of will when the going is smooth is to behave a little like the dypsomaniac who wants to know what sorts of pink rats ordinary people see.[1]

It should be plain now why laughing, if performed as a basic action, is controversial. It is because whoever could so laugh would be positively abnormal, and we cannot understand what he does. In

---

[1] It is not difficult to see why it should be thought that there are two distinct things in the case of trying. It is because we often speak of trying and failing. So, if we can try and also succeed, trying is one thing and succeeding is another. And if succeeding consists in raising an arm, *trying* here must be something different, since failing consists in *not*-raising one's arm, and trying then could hardly consist in raising it. But this is not the important sense of the word for the theory of action.

relation to him, we are in just the same position as the paralytic in relation to us. We lack a kind of gift.

V

It is easy enough to sympathize with those who feel an action is not intelligible unless we can find a causal picture for it. But this is only because they have taken intelligibility to consist in having a causal picture. Dominated by this requirement, they may tend to invent some such picture, populating their inner selves with entities whose job it is to serve the automotive functions demanded by the causal model of intelligibility. But I am asking that we do not strain, and that we use the causal model only where it is natural to use it.

That there are actions, like moving an arm, which do not really require any other action as cause (and so no 'inner' action as a cause) entails, I believe, no refutation of dualism. For all the distinctions I am thinking of are reproduced within the mental world, and cut across the distinction between body and mind. If, for instance, we take the description 'M images I' where I is a mental image, then it is unclear, as it was in the case of 'laughing' or 'moves an arm,' whether M has performed an action or not, or, if an action, then a basic action or not. The whole declension works for, C-1: M may cause an image to appear in his mind, perhaps by taking a drug; C-2: Someone or something other than M may cause an image to appear in M's mind; C-3: M is haunted by an image which appears spontaneously, recurrently, and unpredictably—a symptom, of perhaps a psychic disorder; and C-4: M simply produces an image, as I and all those with the requisite alpha rhythms are able to do, i.e., as a basic action.[1]

I shall not press for a full parity, though I *am* prepared to defend the view that there is a problem of Other Bodies precisely analogous to the problem of Other Minds. All I wish to emphasize is that, whatever disparities there may be between the concept of mind and the concept of body, men may be said to act mentally in much the same way that they may be said to act physically. Among the things I take Descartes to have meant when he said that we are not in our bodies the way a pilot is in a ship, is that we do not always do things, as pilots must with ships, by causing them to happen. We do not turn, as it were, an inner wheel in order, through some elaborate transmission of impulse, to cause an external rudder to shift and, by so doing, get our

[1] But I am not sure whether *we* are positively abnormal, or those who have no images are negatively abnormal.

boat to turn. We act directly. But then neither am I in my *mind* the way a pilot is in a ship. Or rather, I sometimes cause things to happen with my body and with my mind, and I sometimes just act with them directly, as when I perform basic actions. It is best, however, to avoid similes. Any philosophical problems we have with ourselves would only reappear in connexion with anything sufficiently similar to us to be a suitable analogue. But if we find ourselves unintelligible, nothing sufficiently similar to us to be helpful is likely to be more clear.

III

ACTING, WILLING, DESIRING

H. A. PRICHARD

THE question 'What is acting or doing something?' seems at first unreal, i.e. a question to which we already know the answer. For it looks as though everyone knows what doing something is and would be ready to offer instances. No one, for instance, would hesitate to say to another 'You ought to go to bed', on the ground that neither he nor the other knows the kind of thing meant by 'going to bed'. Yet, when we consider instances that would be offered, we do not find it easy to state the common character which we think they had which led us to call them actions.

If, as a preliminary, we look for help to the psychologists, from whom we naturally expect to get it, we find we fail. We find plenty of talk about reflex actions, ideo-motor actions, instinctive actions, and so on, but no discussion of what actions are. Instead, they seem to take for granted that our actions are physical processes taking place within our body, which they certainly are not.

We should at first say that to do something is to originate or to bring into existence, i.e., really, to cause, some not yet existing state either of ourselves or of someone else, or, again, of some body. But, for clearness' sake, we should go on to distinguish those actions in doing which we originated some new state directly from those in which we did this only indirectly, i.e. by originating directly some other state, by originating which we indirectly originated the final state. As instances of the former we might give moving or turning our head, and as instances of the latter, curing our toothache by swallowing aspirin, and killing another by pressing a switch which exploded a charge underneath him. If challenged, however, we should have to allow that even in instances of the former kind we did not originate directly what the instances suggest that we did, since what we did originate directly must have been some new state or states of our nerve-cells, of the nature of which we are ignorant. We should, however, insist that in doing any action we must have originated

From *Moral Obligation* by H. A. Prichard (Clarendon Press, 1949), pp. 187–98. Reprinted by permission of the Clarendon Press.

something directly, since otherwise we could not originate anything indirectly.

The view that to act is to originate something was maintained by Cook Wilson in a paper on *Means and End*. In the course of this paper he also maintained (1) that an action required the desire to do it, and (2) that it is important to avoid the mistake of thinking that the origination of something X is the willing of X, apparently on the ground that if it were, X would exist as soon as we willed it, and yet it usually does not. He also appeared to hold that the origination of X, though not identical with willing the origination, required it, so that when I originated a movement of my hand, this required as an antecedent my willing this origination, and this willing in turn required the desiring to originate the movement.

According to Cook Wilson, then, in considering an action we have to distinguish three things: first, the action itself, the originating something; second, the required willing to originate this; and third, the required desire to originate this. And according to him what we will and what we desire are the same, viz. the action.

Professor Macmurray, in a Symposium[1] on 'What is action?', takes substantially the same view of what an action is. He says: 'An action is not the concomitance of an intention in the mind and an occurrence in the physical world: it is the *producing* of the occurrence by the Self, the *making* of a change in the external world, the *doing* of a deed. No process which terminates in the mind, such as forming an intention, deciding to act, or willing, is either an action or a component of action.' But he goes on to add: 'In certain circumstances such a mental event or process may be followed *necessarily* by action.'

Now, so far as I can see, this account of what an action is, though plausible and having as a truth underlying it that usually in acting we do cause something, is not tenable.

Unquestionably the thing meant by 'an action' is an activity. This is so whether we speak of a man's action in moving his hand, or of a body's action such as that of the heart in pumping the blood, or that of one electron in repelling another. But though we think that some man in moving his hand, or that the sun in attracting the earth, causes a certain movement, we do not think that the man's or the sun's activity *is* or *consists in* causing the movement. And if we ask ourselves: 'Is there such an activity as originating or causing a change in something else?', we have to answer that there is not. To say

[1] Aristotelian Society, Supplementary Volume XVII (1938).

this, of course, is not to say that there is no such thing as causing something, but only to say that though the causing a change may require an activity, it is not itself an activity. If we then ask: 'What is the kind of activity required when one body causes another to move?', we have to answer that we do not know, and that when we speak of a force of attraction or of repulsion we are only expressing our knowledge that there is some activity at work, while being ignorant of what the kind of activity is. In the case, however, of a man, i.e., really, of a man's mind, the matter is different. When, e.g., we think of ourselves as having moved our hand, we are thinking of ourselves as having performed an activity of a certain kind, and, it almost goes without saying, a *mental* activity of a certain kind, an activity of whose nature we were dimly aware in doing the action and of which we can become more clearly aware by reflecting on it. And that we are aware of its special nature is shown by our unhesitatingly distinguishing it from other special mental activities such as thinking, wondering, and imagining. If we ask 'What is the word used for this special kind of activity?' the answer, it seems, has to be 'willing'. (I now think I was mistaken in suggesting that the phrase in use for it is 'setting oneself to cause'.) We also have to admit that while we know the general character of that to which we refer when we use the word 'willing', this character is *sui generis* and so incapable of being defined, i.e. of having its nature expressed in terms of the nature of other things. Even Hume virtually admits this when he says: 'By the *will*, I mean nothing but *the internal impression we feel and are conscious of, when we knowingly give rise to any new motion of our body or new perception of our mind*',[1] and then goes on to add that the impression is impossible to define. Though, however, the activity of willing is indefinable, we can distinguish it from a number of things which it is not. Thus obviously, as Locke insisted, willing is different from desiring, and again, willing is not, as some psychologists would have it, a species of something called conation of which desiring is another species. There is no such genus. Again, it is not, as Green in one passage[2] implies, a species of desiring which is desiring in another sense than that ordinary sense in which we are said to desire while hesitating to act.

In addition, plainly, willing is not resolving, nor attending to a difficult object, as James holds, nor for that matter attending to anything, nor, again, consenting to the reality of what is attended to, as James also maintains, nor, indeed, consenting to anything, nor, once

[1] Hume, *Treatise* (Selby-Bigge, p. 399).
[2] *Prolegomena*; §§ 140–2.

more, identifying ourself with some object of desire, as Green asserts in another passage.[1]

Consequently, there seems to be no resisting the conclusion that where we think of ourselves or of another as having done a certain action, the kind of activity of which we are thinking is that of willing (though we should have to add that we are thinking of our particular act of willing as having been the doing of the action in question, only because we think it caused a certain change), and that when we refer to some instance of this activity, such as our having moved our finger or given some friend a headache, we refer to it thus not because we think it was, or consisted in, the causing our finger to move or our friend's head to ache, but because we think it had a certain change of state as an effect.

If, as it seems we must, we accept this conclusion, that to act is really to will something, we then become faced by the question: 'What sort of thing is it that we will?'

Those who, like Cook Wilson, distinguish between acting and willing, answer that what we will is an action, which according to him is the originating some change. Thus Green says: 'To will an event' (i.e. presumably some change) 'as distinguished from an act is a contradiction.' And by this he seems to mean that, for instance, in the case which he takes of our paying a debt, what we will is the paying of our debt and not our creditor's coming into possession of what we owe him. Again, James and Stout, though they do not consider the question, show by their instances that they take for granted that what we will is an action. Thus James says: 'I will to write, and the act follows. I will to sneeze and it does not.'[2] And Stout illustrates a volition by a man's willing to produce an explosion by applying a lighted match to gunpowder.[3] But, unfortunately, James speaks of what he has referred to as, the act of writing which I will, as certain physiological movements, and similarly Stout speaks of, the production of an explosion which I will, as certain bodily movements. And, of course, the bodily movements to which they are referring are not actions, though they may be the effects of actions. Plainly, then, both are only doing lip-service to the idea that what we will is an action. And James, at least, drops doing even this. For immediately after making the statement just quoted, viz. 'I will to write, and the act follows. I will to sneeze and it does not', he adds: 'I will that

[1] *Prolegomena,* §146.
[2] James, *Psychology,* II, p. 560.
[3] Stout, *Manual of Psychology,* IV, p. 641.

the distant table slide over the floor towards me; it also does not.'
Yet no one would say that the sliding of the table, as distinct from
my sliding it, was an action.

In this connexion it is well for clearness' sake to bear two things
in mind. The first is that some transitive verbs used for particular
actions are also used intransitively. Thus one not only speaks of turning one's head but also says that one's head turned. And the second is
that, while the phrase 'turning one's head' stands for an action and
so for an activity of one's mind, yet when I say 'my head turned' I
am speaking simply of a movement of my head which is a change of
place and not an action. The difference is made clear by considering
what is plainly a mistake made by Professor Macmurray. He says that
the term 'action' is ambiguous. He says: 'It may refer either to what
is done or to the doing of it. It may mean either "doing" or "deed".
When we talk of "an action" we are normally referring to what is
done. . . . To act is to effect a change in the external world. The
deed is the change so effected.' And he emphasizes what he considers
the ambiguity in order to indicate that it is doings and not deeds
that he is considering. Obviously, however, there is no ambiguity
whatever. When I move my hand, the movement of my hand, though
an effect of my action, is not itself an action, and no one who considered the matter would say it was, any more than he would say that the
death of Caesar, as distinct from his murder, was an action or even
part of an action.

This difference between, e.g., my moving my hand and a movement
of my hand, is one which James and Stout seem to ignore, as becomes
obvious when James speaks of the sliding of a table as, like writing,
an action. We find the same thing, too, in Locke. For though, e.g.,
he says that 'we find by experience, that, barely by willing it, we
can move the parts of our bodies',[1] yet in contrasting a human with a
physical action he implies that what we will is a movement of our
body. Probably, if pressed, he would have said that, strictly speaking,
what we will is a movement and so not an action. In addition, James
and Stout seem to treat the distinction between an act of willing, or,
as they prefer to call it, a volition, and what is willed, as if it were
the same as the distinction between an act of willing and its effect,
although they are totally different.

It should be clear from what I have just said that those who hold that
what we will is an action must, to be successful, mean by an action
something which really is an action. They may, of course, maintain

[1] Locke, *Essay*, II. 21, §4.

that what we will is a physical process, such as a movement of my hand, but if they do they are really denying that what we will is an action.

It should also now be clear that if we face the question 'What sort of thing do we will?', we have only two answers to consider: (1) that it is some change of state of some thing or person; and (2) that it is an action. If, however, we are forced to conclude, as we have been, that doing something is an act of willing, we seem forced to exclude the second answer, simply on the ground that if it were true, then whenever we think of ourselves as having done some action, we must be thinking of ourselves as having willed some action, i.e. as having willed the willing of some change X; and to think this seems impossible. By the very nature of willing, it seems, what we will must be something other than willing, so that to will the willing of a change X must be an impossibility. And if we even try to deny this, we find ourselves forced to admit that the willing of X, which (we are contending) is what we will, must in turn really be the willing the willing of something else, and so on, and thus become involved in an infinite regress. It is true that Cook Wilson, in a long unpublished discussion, tried to vindicate the analogous idea that in certain limiting cases, viz. those in which the desire moving us is not the desire of some change but the desire to cause it ourselves, as happens in playing golf or patience, what we originate is identical with our origination of something. But he never seems to me to succeed in meeting the objection that this identity must be impossible. Similarly, it seems to me, it is impossible for there to be a case in which the willing the willing of X is identical with willing X.

We are thus left with the conclusion that where we think we have done some action, e.g. have raised our arm or written a word, what we willed was some change, e.g. some movement of our arm or some movement of ink to a certain place on a piece of paper in front of us. But we have to bear in mind that the change which we willed may not have been the same as the change we think we effected. Thus, where I willed some movement of my second finger, I may at least afterwards think that the change I effected was a movement of my first finger, and, only too often, where I willed the existence of a certain word on a piece of paper, I afterwards find that what I caused was a different word. Again, in two cases of the act we call trying to thread a needle, what I willed may have been the same, though the changes I afterwards think I effected were very different, being in the one case the thread's going through the needle and in the other its passing well outside it.

Suppose now that it be allowed that so far I have been right. Then the following admissions must be made:

1. An action, i.e. a human action, instead of being the originating or causing of some change, is an activity of willing some change, this usually causing some change, and in some cases a physical change, its doing or not doing this depending on the physical conditions of which the agent is largely ignorant.

2. Sometimes, however, we have performed such an activity without, at any rate so far as we know, having caused any physical change. This has happened when, e.g., we willed a movement of our hand, at a time when it was either paralysed or numb with cold, whether we knew this or not. No doubt in such cases our activity would not ordinarily be called an action, but it is of the same sort as what we ordinarily call and think of as an action.

3. There is no reason to limit the change which it is possible to will to a movement of some part of our body, since, as James says in effect, we can just as much will the sliding of a table towards us as a movement of our hand towards our head. Indeed, we may, in fact, will this in order to convince ourselves or someone else that by doing so we shall not cause the table to slide. And it looks as though we sometimes will such things in ordinary life, as when in watching a football match we want some player's speed to increase, and will it to increase.

4. Where we have willed some movement of our body and think we have caused it, we cannot have directly caused it. For what we directly caused, if anything, must have been some change in our brain.

5. Where we think that by willing some change we effected some change in the physical world, we are implying the idea that in doing so, we are butting into, or interfering with, the physical system, just as we think of an approaching comet as effecting a breach in the order of the solar system, so long as we do not regard the comet as part of the system. This idea is, of course, inconsistent with our belief in the uniformity of nature unless we include in nature minds as well as bodies; and in any case it is inconsistent with our belief in the conservation of energy. But so long as we think, as we do, that at any rate on some occasions we really effect something in the physical world, we must admit this. And if we knew that such effecting was impossible, we should give up acting.

We have now to face another question, viz. 'Does acting require a desire, and if it does, the desire of what?'

It is at least very difficult to avoid Aristotle's conclusion that acting requires a desire, if only for the reason he gives, viz. that διάνοια αὐτὴ οὐθὲν κινεῖ. It seems that, as Locke maintained, if we never desired something we should never do anything. But what is the desire required?

Here only one or other of two answers seems possible, viz. (1) that it is a desire of the change X which we will, and (2) that it is a desire of the willing of X. And when we try, we do not find it easy to decide between them. For on the one hand, the desire required seems to have to be the desire of X, on the ground that, if we are to will X, we must desire X. And on the other hand, it seems that it must be the desire to will X, since unless we *desired* to will X we could not will X. Indeed, just for this reason Plato seems to have gone too far in the *Gorgias* when he maintained that in acting we never desire to do what we do, but only that for the sake of which we do it. For, if acting is willing, it seems that the desire required must be a desire of the willing, even though the desire be a dependent desire, i.e. a desire depending on the desire of something else for its own sake, viz. that for the sake of which we do the action. And Plato's mistake seems to have been that of restricting desiring to desiring something for its own sake.

The two answers are, of course, radically different. For if the desire required is the desire of X, the thing desired and the thing willed will be the same, as indeed Green implies that they are when he maintains that willing is desiring in a special sense of 'desiring'. But if so, while the willing of X will require what for want of a better term we seem to have to call the thought of X, as being something involved in the desire of X, it will not require either the desire of the willing of X or, for that reason, even the thought of willing X. On the other hand, if the desire required is the desire to will X, the thing desired and the thing willed will necessarily be different, and while the willing of X will require the desire of willing X and so also the thought of willing X, it will not require the desire of X, though it will require the thought of X, as being something involved in the thought of willing X. It should, however, be noted that in the case of the latter alternative, the desire of X may in some cases be required indirectly as a condition of our desiring the willing of X.

To repeat here for clearness' sake what is central—if the desire required is the desire of X, the willing of X will not require either the desire of the willing of X or even the thought of willing X, while, if the desire required is the desire of willing X, the willing of X will not require the desire of X, though it will require the thought of X.

On consideration, however, we have to reject the idea that the desire required is the desire of X, on three grounds. First, if it were true, we should always will any change which we desired to happen, such as the sliding of the table, whether or not we thought that if we were to will it to happen we should thereby cause it to happen; and obviously we do not. Second, we occasionally will a change to happen without any desire for it to happen. This must occur, e.g., if a man ever does an act moved solely by the desire for revenge, willing, say, the movement of a switch which he is confident will result in the death of another, not from any desire for his death but solely from the desire to cause it by willing the movement. And even if there are no acts animated solely by the desire for revenge, there are certainly actions approximating to this. At all events, in the case of playing a game the desire at work must be not the desire of some change but the desire to cause it. A putter at golf, e.g., has no desire for the ball to fall into the hole; he only desires to cause it to fall in. This contention is, I think, not met by maintaining, as Cook Wilson in fact does, that the player desires the falling into the hole as caused by his action, and so desires the falling as part of, or an element in, his action. Its falling is neither a part of, nor an element in, his action; at best it is only an effect of it. And the player could only be said to desire the falling if, as he does not, he desired it to happen irrespectively of what would cause it to happen. And in this connexion it may be added that if the desire required were the desire of X, it would be impossible to do any act as one which we think would or might fulfil some obligation, since *ex hypothesi* the desire required will be a desire for a change X and not a desire to *will* a change X. Then, third, there is a consideration which comes to light if we consider more closely what it is that we will in certain cases, and more especially in those in which we describe an action as one of trying to do so and so. Suppose, e.g., I have done what we describe as having tried to jump a ditch, and so imply that beforehand I was doubtful of success. Obviously I did not will a movement of my body which I was sure would land me, say, two clear yards on the other side, since if I had thought of willing this I should have realized that willing this would not result in my getting across. I willed that movement the willing of which, if I were to will it, I thought the most likely of all the willings of movements in my power to result in my landing on the farther bank. And in this connexion it seems worth noting that what we call trying to do something is as much doing something as what we ordinarily call doing something, although the word 'trying' suggests that it is not. It is the willing a change described in the way in which I have just described what I willed in trying to jump a ditch.

It therefore seems that the desire required must be the desire of the willing of a certain change X. Yet this conclusion is exposed to two objections. The first is that if it were true, it would be impossible to will something X for the first time. For in this context we mean by a desire to will X a desire we can only have in consequence of thinking that if we were to will X, our doing so would be likely to cause something else, and ultimately something which we desire for its own sake. But we cannot desire to will something X, unless we at least have a conjecture that if we were to will X, our willing X might cause some change which we desire for its own sake. And this conjecture requires the thought that on some previous occasion we have willed X and thence concluded from what we think followed this willing of X that it may have caused something else Y. Yet *ex hypothesi* we cannot have willed X on this previous occasion from the desire to will X, since then we had no idea of what willing X might cause. James expresses what is really this objection, though in a misleading way, when he says: 'If, in voluntary action properly so-called' (i.e. in what is really an action), 'the act must be foreseen, it follows that no creature not endowed with divinatory power can perform an act voluntarily for the first time.'[1] The statement as it stands is, of course, absurd, because no one before acting *knows* what his act will be, or even that he will act. But it can be taken as an inaccurate way of expressing the thought that an act of will requires an idea of something which we may cause if we perform the act.

To this objection I have to confess that I cannot see an answer. Yet I think that there must be an answer, since, however it has come about, for us as we are now an act of will does seem to require the desire of it, and so some idea of something which it might effect. I need hardly add that it is no answer to maintain that the desire immediately required by willing something X is in some cases the desire of X, and in others the desire of willing X.

The second objection is one which seems to me, though insidious, an objection which can be met. It can be stated thus: 'It is all very well to say that the desire immediately presupposed by willing X is the desire to will X. But to say this is not enough. For we often desire to will X, and yet do not, as when we hesitate to get out of bed or out of a warm bath, and when this is so, obviously something else is required, and this something can only be the willing to will X, so that after all there must be such a thing as willing to will.' But to this the reply seems clear. Though it is possible to desire to desire, as when I desire to desire the welfare of my country more than I do, it is impossible to will to will, for the reason already given. And where we hesitate to will X, what is required is not the willing to will X but

[1] James, *Psychology*, II, p. 487.

either a certain increase in our desire to will X or a decrease in our aversion to doing so. Certainly, too, we often act on this idea, hoping, e.g., that by making ourselves think of the coldness of our breakfast if we stay in bed we shall reach a state of desire in which we shall will certain movements of our body. And sometimes we succeed, and when we do, we sometimes, as James puts it, suddenly find that we have got up, the explanation of our surprise apparently being that we, having been absorbed in the process of trying to stimulate our desire to get up, have not reflected on our state of desire and so have not noticed its increase.

There is also to be noticed in this connexion a mistake into which we are apt to fall which leads us to think that there must be such a thing as willing to will. We of course frequently want certain changes to happen and also want to will certain changes. But we are apt not to notice that the objects of these desires differ in respect of the conditions of their realization, and in consequence to carry the account of the process of deliberation described by Aristotle one step too far— as Aristotle did not. According to him, when we want the happening of something Z which is not an action of ours and which we think we cannot cause directly, we often look for something else Y from the happening of which the happening of Z would result, and then if necessary for something else X from the happening of which Y would result, until we come to think of something A from the happening of which X, Y, and Z would in turn result, and which we also think it in our power to cause by a certain act α. And when we have found A the process stops. We, however, are apt to carry the process one step farther, and apply to the act α, i.e. the willing of something β, the willing of which we think likely to cause A, the same process that we applied to Z, Y, X, and A, thus treating the willing of β as if it were not the willing of something (which it is), but a change which some act of willing might cause. As a result of doing this we ask 'From what act of willing would the willing of β result?', and the answer has to be 'The willing the willing of β'. But the very question is mistaken, because the willing of β is not a change like Z, Y, X, and A. The only proper question at this stage must be not 'From what *willing* would the willing of β result?' but 'From what *something* would the willing of β result?' And the proper answer must be: 'From a certain increase in our desire to will β.'

IV

WILLING

A. I. MELDEN

THERE is a difference between my arm rising and my raising my arm, between my muscles moving and my moving my muscles—in short, between a bodily movement or happening and an action. In this paper I examine one attempt to make out the nature of this difference.

Consider the following. Whenever I raise my arm (deliberately, let us say) I bring to pass certain muscle movements: I make these happen. Hence I raise my arm by moving (contracting and expanding) certain muscles of my arm. This, then, is how I raise my arm.

This of course is a bad argument. We cannot identify what one does with what one makes happen. When I flex the biceps brachii of my arm many things are brought to pass, made to happen. Nerve impulses are transmitted to the muscles, neural circuits in the brain are opened and closed, protein molecules in the brain are set into oscillation, and many more things of which I have not the faintest intimation. But let us consider the conclusion on its own merits. Certainly I can contract certain muscles at will. If someone points to the biceps brachii of my arm and asks me to flex it, this I can easily do. So it is tempting to say that when I raise my arm, I do so by moving certain muscles *just as* when I signal, I do so by raising my arm.

But how do I move certain muscles? There is a difference between my biceps becoming flexed and *my* flexing my biceps, just as there is a difference between my arm getting raised and my raising my arm. The flexing of my biceps may occur through no doing of mine (someone might raise my arm and in doing so cause my biceps to be flexed), just as my arm getting raised may be something that happens to me through the action of another person who raises my arm and not through anything I do. And what can the difference be between the occurrence of a muscle movement in my arm and my moving that muscle, except that in the latter case it is by doing something that I bring the muscle

Read at the December, 1959, meeting of the Pacific Division of the American Philosophical Association. Published in *Philosophical Review*, Vol. 69 (1960), pp. 475–84. Reprinted by permission of the author and the *Philosophical Review*.

movement to pass? In short, if it is sensible to say that I raise my arm by moving certain muscles, it is equally sensible to hold that I move those muscles by doing something that brings those muscle movements to pass. And what can this latter doing be that has these muscle movements as effect?

Consider the biceps brachii of my arm. Someone points to it and says, 'Flex it!' What must I do in order to comply? Must I say to myself, 'Move, muscle, move'? If I do this, nothing will happen. Does nothing happen because I do not mean it? Then how do I mean it? 'Meaning what I say'—is this something I do when I say whatever it is that I do say? And how do I do that? Shall we say that I shall mean it only when I *want* my muscle to move? But if I want my biceps to move and stare at it again nothing will happen; I must do something about my want, that is, get what it is that I want. Is it necessary that I set myself—to use H. A. Prichard's expression—to move my biceps?[1] But if 'setting myself' means getting ready, putting myself in a state of readiness, again nothing will happen. And if 'setting myself to do' means trying to do or exerting myself to do, then I need do nothing of the sort. I do not try to raise my arm unless, for example, it is held down—I simply raise it; and I do not try to flex my biceps unless there is some obstacle to be overcome or some chance of failure.

What then is the difference between my muscles being contracted and my contracting my muscles? A familiar doctrine is that in the latter case I will my muscles to move; in the former case there are causes other than the act of volition. So I move my muscles by performing an act of volition which in turn produces a muscle movement.

Grant for a moment that an event labelled 'an act of volition' produces a muscle movement; there is a difference surely between the occurrence of such an event and my producing it. We saw that there is a difference between the occurrence of a muscle movement and my moving that muscle; hence it was that the supposition of acts of volition was invoked. But equally there would seem to be a difference between the occurrence of an act of volition and my performing such an act. Who can say that volitions may not occur through no doing of the subject and in consequence of interior mental events deep within the hidden recesses of the self? If so, willing the muscle movement is not enough; one must will the willing of the muscle movement, and so on ad infinitum. Here someone may

[1] Cf. the essay 'Duty and Ignorance of Fact' in *Moral Obligation* (Oxford, 1949).

retort impatiently: 'When I will a muscle movement, *I* will it and that is the end of the matter; there is no other doing by virtue of which this act of volition gets done—I simply will the movement.' But even if this reply were correct it would not serve to explain what an action is, as distinguished from a mere happening. It explains the 'action' of raising the arm in terms of an internal action of willing, and hence all it does at best is to change the locus of action. Indeed it invites the view argued by Prichard that, strictly speaking and contrary to the notion conveyed by our ordinary ways of speaking, one does not raise one's arm at all: all one does or can do is will and by means of this action produce various effects such as the rising of one's arm. In any case if willing is some sort of doing which one performs not by means of any other doing—one wills and that is the end of the matter—why not say the same with respect to the muscle movement itself, or the tensing of one's biceps? One simply tenses it and there is no doing by virtue of which the tensing gets done. But the troubles involved in the supposition that there are interior acts of willing go even deeper than this; the doctrine, familiar though it may be, is a mare's nest of confusions.

How shall we describe the alleged action of willing? Surely a description of this action independently of the consequence alleged for it—the production of a muscle movement—must be forthcoming. Let us call the act of willing *A*; then *A* produces *B* (a muscle movement), this being taken to be a causal sequence. Now in general if *A* causes *B*, a description of *A* other than that it has the causal property of producing *B* must be forthcoming; otherwise '*A* causes *B*' degenerates into 'the thing that produces *B* produces *B*'. But what description of the act of volition can be offered? If something causes me to jump in fright, jerk my arm, or move my head, 'What caused you to . . . ?' is intelligible and answerable. It is no good saying, 'That which caused me to do it', for this is no answer but a bit of rudeness or a feeble attempt at humour. How then shall one describe the act of willing?

It is at this point that the resort to indefinables appears attractive.[1] Willing is *sui generis*, indefinable, a bit of mental self-exertion in which we engage, an activity not capable of further description but different from the wonderings, thinkings, supposings, expectings, picturings,

[1] Indeed, this is the move made by Prichard in the essay 'Acting, Willing, Desiring', written in 1945 and published posthumously in *Moral Obligation* (Oxford, 1949). This essay is worth careful reading; in it Prichard abandons his earlier account of 'willing' as setting oneself to do. [The essay is reprinted in this volume, pp. 59–69. Ed.]

and so forth, that comprise our mental activities. Yet the appeal to indefinables is a desperate defence that purchases immunity from further attack only at the expense of unintelligibility. If all that can be said about the alleged act of volition by virtue of which a muscle movement is produced is that it is the sort of thing that produces a muscle movement, there is every uncertainty that anyone has understood what is meant by 'the act of volition'. And if an attempt to rescue this doctrine is made by appealing to something with which, it is alleged, each of us is intimately familiar and hence will have no difficulty in recognizing—the act of volition that produces the muscle movement—the retort must surely be '*What* do I recognize when I recognize an act of volition?' Unless I can recognize this act by having some description in mind that applies to such acts and only to these, it is at best a simple begging of the question to insist that all of us really understand what is being referred to; in fact, it is an implied charge of dishonesty directed at those who refuse to give their assent. And in philosophy, when good manners alone stand in the way of the open parade of charges of this sort, there is something seriously amiss in one's thinking.

But the difficulty in this talk about acts of volition is not merely that some account of acts of volition in general is needed, failing which we can only conclude that the expression 'act of volition' can play no role in our discourse, it is equally serious in other respects as well. Let us grant that there is some peculiar mental activity of willing the causal consequence of which is that certain muscles are contracted and others relaxed as we perform our diverse bodily movements, and let us now ask first of all how it is that we are able to learn how to perform these bodily movements. Surely the act of volition involved in the production of one muscle movement must be distinguished from the act of volition involved in the production of any other. There will then be different acts of volition, v_1, v_2, v_3, and so forth, which, respectively, move muscles m_1, m_2, m_3, and so forth. If $v_1 \rightarrow m_1$, $v_2 \rightarrow m_2$, $v_3 \rightarrow m_3$, and so forth, represent causal relations, then just as m_1, m_2, m_3 are distinguishable, so v_1, v_2, v_3 will needs be different in kind. And if I am to learn how to produce m_1 by performing the act of volition v_1, I must not only recognize the difference between v_1 and other acts of volition that have other effects; I must also recognize the causal relation holding between v_1 and m_1. Now this would seem to imply at least two things: (1) It must be possible to offer a set of characterizations of these acts of volition each different from the other, corresponding to the set of characterizations that can be given, surely, for the muscle movements m_1, m_2, m_3, m_4, and so forth. (2) I can learn only from experience that m_1 is produced by v_1, m_2 by v_2, m_3 by v_3, and so on. Hence, unless I suppose myself to have been endowed with superhuman prescience, I cannot but have been surprised or astonished the first time I performed the act of volition v_1 to discover that muscle movement m_1 occurred, and antecedently I should have no reason for ruling out the possibility that m_2 would occur; I should have no reason, for example, to suppose that when I performed the act of volition by which in fact my biceps became flexed, my right leg would not have been raised.

Consider the first of these consequences. Now I can certainly distinguish between muscle movements m_1 and m_2, say, the biceps of my right arm from that of my left arm. But how shall I distinguish between the acts of volition v_1 and v_2 by which these distinct muscle movements are produced? If I produce these muscle movements by performing these acts of volition, this at any rate is something I learn to do, an ability I come to acquire. But if I can learn to do this, I must be able to distinguish between the volitions v_1 and v_2. Surely it must be possible to describe the difference. And if this cannot be done, learning to produce m_1 by producing v_1 and learning to produce m_2 by producing v_2 is impossible. How then shall we describe v_1 as distinguished from v_2? Shall we say that not only are volitions in general indefinable, but that the difference between v_1 and v_2 is also something indefinable? At least, however, the difference must be recognizable. Is it that our vocabulary is inadequate? Then let us introduce words that will enable us to mark the distinction. And now that the words have been introduced, explain how they are to be employed! Is it that we can only *point*: v_1 is *this* thing, the one that one finds one performs when m_1 is produced, v_2 is *that* thing, the one that one finds that one performs when m_2 is produced? But this will do the trick only if I already know what sorts of things to look for and only if it is at least possible for me to go on and describe the difference between v_1 and v_2 independently of the considerations that v_1 produces m_1 and v_2 produces m_2. By pointing one can succeed in explaining the meaning of a term or expression, but only if by doing so one can help fill in a gap or supply the links missing in some initial background understanding we have of that term or expression. But here we do not know where to look or what to find. No background understanding is present; we are told that there are certain things—call them 'acts of volition'—that they are indefinable, and that nothing more can be said about them at all in explaining how this expression 'act of volition' is to be employed. Against this background, how can pointing serve to provide any explanation at all of the difference between act of volition$_1$ (call it mental-muscle-doing$_1$) and act of volition$_2$ (mental-muscle-doing$_2$)? To say at this point that the difference itself is indefinable is, surely, to carry philosophical pretension beyond all limits of credulity.

As far as I know, philosophers are quite unwilling to pile indefinables upon indefinables in this fulsome manner. Prichard for one, despite his characteristic resort to indefinables, is admirable for an equally characteristic subtlety that leads him to reject such simple-minded answers even though, as he himself recognizes, he must accept a conclusion that is open to objections he cannot meet. Consider the second of the two consequences of the doctrine of acts of volition. That v_1 produces m_1 rather than m_2 is a causal fact; but if so, I should have no reason to suppose, when I first performed the act of volition v_1 that m_1 rather than m_2 would follow; for on this view the statement that, for example, I move the biceps brachii of my right arm by performing the act of volition v_1, rather than the biceps brachii of my left arm or the biceps femoris of my right leg, is justified only on the basis of inductive evidence. Now Prichard holds that an act of volition involves a desire to will whatever it is that one wills, and hence some idea of what the volition is likely to produce. This, however, is impossible on the present view since on the first occasion on which I performed v_1 and thereby produced m_1, v_1 would require the thought that I would be doing something that would produce m_1 and by hypothesis I should have no reason to expect what, if anything, v_1 would produce. Prichard is therefore led to the conclusion that an 'act of will requires an idea of something which we may cause if we perform the act', a conclusion—indeed a difficulty—he is unable to avoid.[1]

Prichard's predicament involves a matter of central importance which can be stated quite independently of his insistence that if one is to perform an act of volition, one must be moved by a desire to perform that act of volition. The important issue raised by Prichard is whether or not it is intelligible to speak of an act of volition where the very notion of such an act does not involve a reference to the relevant bodily event. Let the act of volition issue in a muscle movement, then, as Prichard himself recognizes, the act must be the

[1] Op. cit., pp. 196–197. [p. 68 of this volume, Ed.]. See also his second thoughts about his earlier notion of 'setting oneself' in the footnotes to his earlier essay, 'Duty and Ignorance of Fact', which appear in the same volume (p. 38).

willing of that muscle movement; otherwise we should have only inductive grounds for supposing the act to issue in that particular muscle movement. Accordingly we are faced with the following dilemma: If in thinking of v_1 (some particular act of volition) we are of necessity to think of it as the willing of m_1 (some particular muscle movement), then v_1 cannot be any occurrence, mental or physiological, which is causally related to m_1, since the very notion of a causal sequence logically implies that cause and effect are intelligible without any logically internal relation of the one to the other. If, on the other hand, we think of v_1 and m_1 as causally related in the way in which we think of the relation between the movements of muscles and the raising of one's arm, then we must conclude that when first we perform v_1 we should be taken completely by surprise to find that m_1 does in fact ensue. If to avoid this latter consequence we maintain that the thought of the muscle movement enters into the very character of the act of volition (as Prichard puts it, 'the *thinking* enters into the character of the *willing*'[1]), no description of the act of volition can be given that does not involve an account of the muscle movement, and hence we must abandon the idea that the act of volition v_1 is a cause that produces m_1, the muscle movement. Prichard's predicament is that his conclusion that 'an act of will requires an idea of something which we may cause if we perform the act' is nothing less than self-contradictory.

This then is the logical incoherence involved in the doctrine of acts of volition. Acts of volition are alleged to be direct causes of certain bodily phenomena (whether these be brain occurrences, as Prichard supposed them to be, or muscle movements, as we have been assuming for the sake of argument, is of no matter) just as the latter are causes of the raising of one's arm. For, it is alleged, just as we raise our arms by moving our muscles, so we move our muscles by willing them to move. But no account of the alleged volitions is intelligible that does not involve a reference to the relevant bodily phenomena. And no interior cause, mental or physiological, can have this logical feature of acts of volition. Let the interior event which we call 'the act of volition' be mental or physical (which it is will make no difference at all), it must be logically distinct from the alleged effect: this surely is one lesson we can derive from a reading of Hume's discussion of causation. Yet nothing can be an act of volition that is not logically connected with that which is willed; the act of willing

[1]Ibid, p. 38

is intelligible only as the act of willing whatever it is that is willed. In short, there could not be such an interior event like an act of volition since (here one is reminded of Wittgenstein's famous remark about meaning) nothing of that sort could have the required logical consequences.

Let me review the course of the argument. The doctrine of acts of volition was introduced, it will be remembered, in order to elucidate the distinction between one's arm rising and one's raising one's arm. The former need involve no doing or action performed by the agent; the latter surely does. But instead of rejecting the question 'How does one raise one's arm?' by a 'One just does' retort, the reply we considered was 'One raises one's arm by moving certain muscles'. Here the same question arises again: how can one distinguish between 'moving certain muscles' and 'certain muscles getting moved'? The latter need involve no action on my part at all. And if it makes sense to ask, 'How does one raise one's arm?' surely it makes sense to ask, 'How does one move certain muscles?' Hence the doing required in order to preserve the distinction between 'moving certain muscles' and 'certain muscles getting moved' must be a doing other than the doing described as 'moving certain muscles.' At this point the philosophical doctrine of acts of volition—willings performed by an agent—appears attractive. By willing we move certain muscles; by moving certain muscles we raise our arm. But the acts of volition in question are the ill-begotten offspring of the mating of two quite incompatible ideas: the supposition that such acts are causes, and the requirement that the volitions in question be the willings of the muscle movements. As causes, willings are events on a par with other events including muscle and other bodily movements, with respect to which the inevitable question must arise once more: 'How does one perform such an action?' since after all there is the distinction to be preserved between 'performing a willing' and 'a willing occurring'. But if to avoid the threatened regress of 'willing a willing' and 'willing the willing of a willing' and so on, one rejects the question and questions the intelligibility of such locutions as 'willing a willing', the willing in question can only be understood as 'the willing of a muscle movement'. If so, the willing in question cannot be a cause of the muscle movement, since the reference to the muscle movement is involved in the very description of the willing. In that case to say that one moves certain muscles by willing them to move is not to give any causal account at all. But if this is so, what can it mean to say that one wills a muscle movement—since the willing in question cannot possibly be any interior occurrence in which one engages? If it is intelligible at all it means simply that one moves a muscle. In that case, the alleged elucidation of the statement that one moves certain muscles (in raising one's arm) by willing them to move degenerates into something that is no elucidation at all, namely, that one moves certain muscles by moving them. And if this is so, to say that one wills the movement of certain muscles is not to answer the question 'How does one move those muscles?'; it is in fact to reject it. If this is the outcome, why not refuse to plunge into the morass and reject the initial question 'How does one raise one's arm?' by saying 'One just does?' If, on the other hand, 'willing a muscle movement' does not mean 'moving a muscle', what on earth can it possibly mean? Surely it is an understatement to say that the philosophical talk about acts of volition involves a mare's nest of confusions!

It is not my contention that the doctrine of volitions is designed to answer only those questions I have raised so far. It is of course true that frequently this doctrine is also invoked in order to give some account of the difference between action that is voluntary and action that is not. Nor do I deny that there is any legitimacy in our familiar use of such locutions as 'acting willingly', 'doing something of one's own will', 'acting wilfully', and so on. But these are matters to be examined in their own right and at the proper time.

V

ACTIONS, REASONS, AND CAUSES

Donald Davidson

WHAT is the relation between a reason and an action when the reason explains the action by giving the agent's reason for doing what he did? We may call such explanations *rationalizations*, and say that the reason *rationalizes* the action.

In this paper I want to defend the ancient—and common-sense—position that rationalization is a species of ordinary causal explanation. The defence no doubt requires some redeployment, but not more or less complete abandonment of the position, as urged by many recent writers.[1]

I

A reason rationalizes an action only if it leads us to see something the agent saw, or thought he saw, in his action—some feature, consequence, or aspect of the action the agent wanted, desired, prized, held dear, thought dutiful, beneficial, obligatory, or agreeable. We cannot explain why someone did what he did simply by saying the particular action appealed to him; we must indicate what it was about the action that appealed. Whenever someone does something for a reason, therefore, he can be characterized as (*a*) having some sort of pro attitude toward actions of a certain kind, and (*b*) believing (or knowing, perceiving, noticing, remembering) that his action is of that kind. Under (*a*) are to be included desires, wantings, urges,

Presented in a symposium on 'Action' at the sixtieth annual meeting of the American Philosophical Association, December 29, 1963. Published in *Journal of Philosophy*, Vol. 60 (1963), pp. 685–700. © 1963 by Journal of Philosophy, Inc. Reprinted by permission of the author and the *Journal of Philosophy*.

[1]Some examples: G. E. M. Anscombe, *Intention*, Oxford, 1959; Stuart Hampshire, *Thought and Action*, London, 1959; H. L. A. Hart and A. M. Honoré, *Causation in the Law*, Oxford, 1959; William Dray, *Laws and Explanation in History*, Oxford, 1957; and most of the books in the series edited by R. F. Holland, *Studies in Philosophical Psychology*, including Anthony Kenny, *Action, Emotion and Will*, London, 1963, and A. I. Melden, *Free Action*, London, 1961. Page references in parentheses will all be to these works.

promptings, and a great variety of moral views, aesthetic principles, economic prejudices, social conventions, and public and private goals and values in so far as these can be interpreted as attitudes of an agent directed toward actions of a certain kind. The word 'attitude' does yeoman service here, for it must cover not only permanent character traits that show themselves in a lifetime of behaviour, like love of children or a taste for loud company, but also the most passing fancy that prompts a unique action, like a sudden desire to touch a woman's elbow. In general, pro attitudes must not be taken for convictions, however temporary, that every action of a certain kind ought to be performed, is worth performing, or is, all things considered, desirable. On the contrary, a man may all his life have a yen, say, to drink a can of paint, without ever, even at the moment he yields, believing it would be worth doing.

Giving the reason why an agent did something is often a matter of naming the pro attitude (*a*) or the related belief (*b*) or both; let me call this pair the *primary reason* why the agent performed the action. Now it is possible to reformulate the claim that rationalizations are causal explanations, and give structure to the argument as well, by stating two theses about primary reasons:

1. For us to understand how a reason of any kind rationalizes an action it is necessary and sufficient that we see, at least in essential outline, how to construct a primary reason.

2. The primary reason for an action is its cause.

I shall argue for these points in turn.

II

I flip the switch, turn on the light, and illuminate the room. Unbeknownst to me I also alert a prowler to the fact that I am home. Here I do not do four things, but only one, of which four descriptions have been given.[1] I flipped the switch because I wanted to turn on

[1] We would not call my unintentional alerting of the prowler an action, but it should not be inferred from this that alerting the prowler is therefore something different from flipping the switch, say just its consequence. Actions, performances, and events not involving intention are alike in that they are often referred to or defined partly in terms of some terminal stage, outcome, or consequence.

The word 'action' does not very often occur in ordinary speech, and when it does it is usually reserved for fairly portentous occasions. I follow a useful philosophical practice in calling anything an agent does intentionally an action, including intentional omissions. What is really needed is some suitably generic

the light, and by saying I wanted to turn on the light I explain (give my reason for, rationalize) the flipping. But I do not, by giving this reason, rationalize my alerting of the prowler nor my illuminating of the room. Since reasons may rationalize what someone does when it is described in one way and not when it is described in another, we cannot treat what was done simply as a term in sentences like 'My reason for flipping the switch was that I wanted to turn on the light'; otherwise we would be forced to conclude, from the fact that flipping the switch was identical with alerting the prowler, that my reason for alerting the prowler was that I wanted to turn on the light. Let us mark this quasi-intensional[1] character of action descriptions in rationalizations by stating a bit more precisely a necessary condition for primary reasons:

C1. *R* is a primary reason why an agent performed the action *A* under the description *d* only if *R* consists of a pro attitude of the agent toward actions with a certain property, and a belief of the agent that *A*, under the description *d*, has that property.

How can my wanting to turn on the light be (part of) a primary reason, since it appears to lack the required element of generality? We may be taken in by the verbal parallel between 'I turned on the light' and 'I wanted to turn on the light'. The first clearly refers to a particular event, so we conclude that the second has this same event as its object. Of course it is obvious that the event of my turning on the light can't be referred to in the same way by both sentences, since the existence of the event is required by the truth of 'I turned on the light' but not by the truth of 'I wanted to turn on the light'. If the reference were the same in both cases, the second sentence would entail the first; but in fact the sentences are logically independent. What is less obvious, at least until we attend to it, is that the event whose occurrence makes 'I turned on the light' true cannot be called

term to bridge the following gap: suppose '*A*' is a description of an action, '*B*' is a description of something done voluntarily, though not intentionally, and '*C*' is a description of something done involuntarily and unintentionally; finally, suppose $A = B = C$. Then *A*, *B*, and *C* are the same—what? 'Action', 'event', 'thing done', each have, at least in some contexts, a strange ring when coupled with the wrong sort of description. Only the question 'Why did you (he) do *A*?' has the true generality required. Obviously, the problem is greatly aggravated if we assume, as Melden does (*Free Action*, 85), that an action ('raising one's arm') can be identical with a bodily movement ('one's arm going up').

[1] 'Quasi-intensional' because, besides its intensional aspect, the description of the action must also refer in rationalizations; otherwise it could be true that an action was done for a certain reason and yet the action not have been performed. Compare 'the author of *Waverley*' in 'George IV knew the author of *Waverley* wrote *Waverley*'.

the object, however intensional, of 'I wanted to turn on the light'. If I turned on the light, then I must have done it at a precise moment, in a particular way—every detail is fixed. But it makes no sense to demand that my want be directed at an action performed at any one moment or done in some unique manner. Any one of an indefinitely large number of actions would satisfy the want, and can be considered equally eligible as its object. Wants and desires often are trained on physical objects. However, 'I want that gold watch in the window' is not a primary reason, and explains why I went into the store only because it suggests a primary reason—for example, that I wanted to buy the watch.

Because 'I wanted to turn on the light' and 'I turned on the light' are logically independent, the first can be used to give a reason why the second is true. Such a reason gives minimal information: it implies that the action was intentional, and wanting tends to exclude some other pro attitudes, such as a sense of duty or obligation. But the exclusion depends very much on the action and the context of explanation. Wanting seems pallid beside lusting, but it would be odd to deny that someone who lusted after a woman or a cup of coffee wanted her or it. It is not unnatural, in fact, to treat wanting as a genus including all pro attitudes as species. When we do this and when we know some action is intentional, it is empty to add that the agent wanted to do it. In such cases, it is easy to answer the question 'Why did you do it?' with 'For no reason', meaning not that there is no reason but that there is no *further* reason, no reason that cannot be inferred from the fact that the action was done intentionally; no reason, in other words, besides wanting to do it. This last point is not essential to the present argument, but it is of interest because it defends the possibility of defining an intentional action as one done for a reason.

A primary reason consists of a belief and an attitude, but it is generally otiose to mention both. If you tell me you are easing the jib because you think that will stop the main from backing, I don't need to be told that you want to stop the main from backing; and if you say you are biting your thumb at me because you want to insult me, there is no point in adding that you think that by biting your thumb at me you will insult me. Similarly, many explanations of actions in terms of reasons that are not primary do not require mention of the primary reason to complete the story. If I say I am pulling weeds because I want a beautiful lawn, it would be fatuous to eke out the account with 'And so I see something desirable in any action that does, or has a good chance of, making the lawn beautiful'. Why insist that there is any *step*, logical or psychological, in the transfer of desire from an end that is not an action to the actions one conceives as means? It serves the argument as well that the desired end explains the action only if what are believed by the agent to be means are desired.

Fortunately, it is not necessary to classify and analyse the many varieties of emotions, sentiments, moods, motives, passions, and hungers whose mention may answer the question 'Why did you do it?' in order to see how, when such mention rationalizes the action, a primary reason is involved. Claustrophobia gives a man's reason for leaving a cocktail party because we know people want to avoid, escape from, be safe from, put distance between themselves and, what they fear. Jealousy is the motive in a poisoning because, among other things, the poisoner believes his action will harm his rival, remove the cause of his agony, or redress an injustice, and these are the sorts of things a jealous man wants to do. When we learn a man cheated his son out of greed, we do not necessarily know what the primary reason was, but we know there was one, and its general nature. Ryle analyses 'he boasted from vanity' into "he boasted on meeting the stranger and his doing so satisfies the lawlike proposition that whenever he finds a chance of securing the admiration and envy of others, he does whatever he thinks will produce this admiration and envy" (*The Concept of Mind*, 89). This analysis is often, and perhaps justly, criticized on the ground that a man may boast from vanity just once. But if Ryle's boaster did what he did from vanity, then something entailed by Ryle's analysis is true: the boaster wanted to secure the admiration and envy of others, and he believed that his action would produce this admiration and envy; true or false, Ryle's analysis does not dispense with primary reasons, but depends upon them.

To know a primary reason why someone acted as he did is to know an intention with which the action was done. If I turn left at the fork because I want to get to Katmandu, my intention in turning left is to get to Katmandu. But to know the intention is not necessarily to know the primary reason in full detail. If James goes to church with the intention of pleasing his mother, then he must have some pro attitude toward pleasing his mother, but it needs more information to tell whether his reason is that he enjoys pleasing his mother, or thinks it right, his duty, or an obligation. The expression 'the intention with which James went to church' has the outward form of a description, but in fact it is syncategorematic and cannot be taken to refer to an entity, state, disposition, or event. Its function in context is to generate new descriptions of actions in terms of their reasons; thus 'James went to church with the intention of pleasing his mother' yields a new, and fuller, description of the action described in 'James went to church'. Essentially the same process goes on when I answer the question 'Why are you bobbing around that way?' with 'I'm knitting, weaving, exercising, sculling, cuddling, training fleas'.

Straight description of an intended result often explains an action better than stating that the result was intended or desired. 'It will soothe your nerves' explains why I pour you a shot as efficiently as 'I want to do something to soothe your nerves', since the first in the context of explanation implies the second; but the first does better, because, if it is true, the facts will justify my choice of action. Because justifying and explaining an action so often go hand in hand, we frequently indicate the primary reason for an action by making a claim which, if true, would also verify, vindicate, or support the relevant belief or attitude of the agent. 'I knew I ought to return it', 'The paper said it was going to snow', 'You stepped on *my* toes', all, in appropriate reason-giving contexts, perform this familiar dual function.

The justifying role of a reason, given this interpretation, depends upon the explanatory role, but the converse does not hold. Your stepping on my toes neither explains nor justifies my stepping on your toes unless I believe you stepped on my toes, but the belief alone, true or false, explains my action.

III

In the light of a primary reason, an action is revealed as coherent with certain traits, long- or short-termed, characteristic or not, of the agent, and the agent is shown in his role of Rational Animal. Corresponding to the belief and attitude of a primary reason for an action, we can always construct (with a little ingenuity) the premises of a syllogism from which it follows that the action has some (as Miss Anscombe calls it) "desirability characteristic".[1] Thus there is a

[1] Miss Anscombe denies that the practical syllogism is deductive. This she does partly because she thinks of the practical syllogism, as Aristotle does, as corresponding to a piece of practical reasoning (whereas for me it is only part of the analysis of the concept of a reason with which someone acted), and therefore she is bound, again following Aristotle, to think of the conclusion of a practical syllogism as corresponding to a judgement, not merely that the action has a desirable characteristic, but that the action is desirable (reasonable, worth doing, etc.).

certain irreducible—though somewhat anaemic—sense in which every rationalization justifies: from the agent's point of view there was, when he acted, something to be said for the action.

Noting that nonteleological causal explanations do not display the element of justification provided by reasons, some philosophers have concluded that the concept of cause that applies elsewhere cannot apply to the relation between reasons and actions, and that the pattern of justification provides, in the case of reasons, the required explanation. But suppose we grant that reasons alone justify in explaining actions; it does not follow that the explanation is not also—and necessarily—causal. Indeed our first condition for primary reasons (C1) is designed to help set rationalizations apart from other sorts of explanation. If rationalization is, as I want to argue, a species of causal explanation, then justification, in the sense given by C1, is at least one differentiating property. How about the other claim: that justifying is a kind of explaining, so that the ordinary notion of cause need not be brought in? Here it is necessary to decide what is being included under justification. Perhaps it means only what is given by C1: that the agent has certain beliefs and attitudes in the light of which the action is reasonable. But then something essential has certainly been left out, for a person can have a reason for an action, and perform the action, and yet this reason not be the reason why he did it. Central to the relation between a reason and an action it explains is the idea that the agent performed the action *because* he had the reason. Of course, we can include this idea too in justification; but then the notion of justification becomes as dark as the notion of reason until we can account for the force of that 'because'.

When we ask why someone acted as he did, we want to be provided with an interpretation. His behaviour seems strange, alien, outré, pointless, out of character, disconnected; or perhaps we cannot even recognize an action in it. When we learn his reason, we have an interpretation, a new description of what he did which fits it into a familiar picture. The picture certainly includes some of the agent's beliefs and attitudes; perhaps also goals, ends, principles, general character traits, virtues or vices. Beyond this, the redescription of an action afforded by a reason may place the action in a wider social, economic, linguistic, or evaluative context. To learn, through learning the reason, that the agent conceived his action as a lie, a repayment of a debt, an insult, the fulfilment of an avuncular obligation, or a knight's gambit is to grasp the point of the action in its setting of rules, practices, conventions, and expectations.

Remarks like these, inspired by the later Wittgenstein, have been elaborated with subtlety and insight by a number of philosophers. And there is no denying that this is true: when we explain an action, by giving the reason, we do redescribe the action; redescribing the action gives the action a place in a pattern, and in this way the action is explained. Here it is tempting to draw two conclusions that do not follow. First, we can't infer, from the fact that giving reasons merely redescribes the action and that causes are separate from effects, that therefore reasons are not causes. Reasons, being beliefs and attitudes, are certainly not identical with actions; but, more important, events are often redescribed in terms of their causes. (Suppose someone was injured. We could redescribe this event 'in terms of a cause' by saying he was burned.) Second, it is an error to think that, because placing the action in a larger pattern explains it, therefore we now understand the sort of explanation involved. Talk of patterns and contexts does not answer the question of how reasons explain actions, since the relevant pattern or context contains both reason and action. One way we can explain an event is by placing it in the context of its cause; cause and effect form the sort of pattern that explains the effect, in a sense of 'explain' that we understand as well as any. If reason and action illustrate a different pattern of explanation, that pattern must be identified.

Let me urge the point in connexion with an example of Melden's. A man driving an automobile raises his arm in order to signal. His intention, to signal, explains his action, raising his arm, by redescribing it as signalling. What is the pattern that explains the action? Is it the familiar pattern of an action done for a reason? Then it does indeed explain the action, but only because it assumes the relation of reason and action that we want to analyse. Or is the pattern rather this: the man is driving, he is approaching a turn; he knows he ought to signal; he knows how to signal, by raising his arm. And now, in this context, he raises his arm. Perhaps, as Melden suggests, if all this happens, he does signal. And the explanation would then be this: if, under these conditions, a man raises his arm, then he signals. The difficulty is, of course, that this explanation does not touch the question of why he raised his arm. He had a reason to raise his arm, but this has not been shown to be the reason why he did it. If the description 'signalling' explains his action by giving his reason, then the signalling must be intentional; but, on the account just given, it may not be.

If, as Melden claims, causal explanations are 'wholly irrelevant to the understanding we seek' of human actions (184) then we are without an analysis of the 'because' in 'He did it because . . .', where we go on to name a reason. Hampshire remarks, of the relation between reasons and action, 'In philosophy one ought surely to find this . . . connection altogether mysterious' (166). Hampshire rejects Aristotle's attempt to solve the mystery by introducing the concept of wanting as a causal factor, on the grounds that the resulting theory is too clear and definite to fit all cases and that 'There is still no compelling ground for insisting that the word "want" *must* enter into every full statement of reasons for acting' (168). I agree that the concept of wanting is too narrow, but I have argued that, at least in a vast number of typical cases, some pro attitude must be assumed to be present if a statement of an agent's reasons in acting is to be intelligible. Hampshire does not see how Aristotle's scheme can be appraised as true or false, 'for it is not clear what could be the basis of assessment, or what kind of evidence could be decisive' (167). Failing a satisfactory alternative, the best argument for a scheme like Aristotle's is that it alone promises to give an account of the 'mysterious connection' between reasons and actions.

IV

In order to turn the first 'and' to 'because' in 'He exercised *and* he wanted to reduce and thought exercise would do it', we must, as the basic move,[1] augment condition C_1 with:

C_2. A primary reason for an action is its cause.

The considerations in favour of C_2 are by now, I hope, obvious; in the remainder of this paper I wish to defend C_2 against various lines of attack and, in the process, to clarify the notion of causal explanation involved.

A. The first line of attack is this. Primary reasons consist of attitudes and beliefs, which are states or dispositions, not events; therefore they cannot be causes.

It is easy to reply that states, dispositions, and conditions are frequently named as the causes of events: the bridge collapsed because of a structural defect; the plane crashed on take-off because the air

---

[1] I say 'as the basic move' to cancel the suggestion that C_1 and C_2 are jointly *sufficient* to define the relation of reasons to the actions they explain. I believe C_2 can be strengthened to make C_1 and C_2 sufficient as well as necessary conditions, but here I am concerned only with the claim that both are, as they stand, necessary.

temperature was abnormally high; the plate broke because it had a crack. This reply does not, however, meet a closely related point. Mention of a causal condition for an event gives a cause only on the assumption that there was also a preceding event. But what is the preceding event that causes an action?

In many cases it is not difficult at all to find events very closely associated with the primary reason. States and dispositions are not events, but the onslaught of a state or disposition is. A desire to hurt your feelings may spring up at the moment you anger me; I may start wanting to eat a melon just when I see one; and beliefs may begin at the moment we notice, perceive, learn, or remember something. Those who have argued that there are no mental events to qualify as causes of actions have often missed the obvious because they have insisted that a mental event be observed or noticed (rather than an observing or a noticing) or that it be like a stab, a qualm, a prick or a quiver, a mysterious prod of conscience or act of the will. Melden, in discussing the driver who signals a turn by raising his arm, challenges those who want to explain actions causally to identify 'an event which is common and peculiar to all such cases' (87), perhaps a motive or an intention, anyway 'some particular feeling or experience' (95). But of course there is a mental event: at some moment the driver noticed (or thought he noticed) his turn coming up, and that is the moment he signalled. During any continuing activity, like driving, or elaborate performance, like swimming the Hellespont, there are more or less fixed purposes, standards, desires, and habits that give direction and form to the entire enterprise, and there is the continuing input of information about what we are doing, about changes in the environment, in terms of which we regulate and adjust our actions. To dignify a driver's awareness that his turn has come by calling it an experience, much less a feeling, is no doubt exaggerated, but whether it deserves a name or not, it had better be the reason why he raises his arm. In this case, and typically, there may not be anything we would call a motive, but if we mention such a general purpose as wanting to get to one's destination safely, it is clear that the motive is not an event. The intention with which the driver raises his arm is also not an event, for it is no thing at all, neither event, attitude, disposition, nor object. Finally, Melden asks the causal theorist to find an event that is common and peculiar to all cases where a man intentionally raises his arm, and this, it must be admitted, cannot be produced. But then neither can a common and unique cause of bridge failures, plane crashes, or plate breakings be produced.

The signalling driver can answer the question 'Why did you raise your arm when you did?', and from the answer we learn the event that caused the action. But can an actor always answer such a question? Sometimes the answer will mention a mental event that does not give a reason: 'Finally I made up my mind'. However, there also seem to be cases of intentional action where we cannot explain at all why we acted when we did. In such cases, explanation in terms of primary reasons parallels the explanation of the collapse of the bridge from a structural defect: we are ignorant of the event or sequence of events that led up to (caused) the collapse, but we are sure there was such an event or sequence of events.

B. According to Melden, a cause must be 'logically distinct from the alleged effect' (52); but a reason for an action is not logically distinct from the action; therefore, reasons are not causes of actions.[1]

One possible form of this argument has already been suggested. Since a reason makes an action intelligible by redescribing it, we do not have two events, but only one under different descriptions. Causal relations, however, demand distinct events.

Someone might be tempted into the mistake of thinking that my flipping of the switch caused my turning on of the light (in fact it caused the light to go on). But it does not follow that it is a mistake to take 'My reason for flipping the switch was that I wanted to turn on the light' as entailing, in part, 'I flipped the switch, and this action is further describable as having been caused by my wanting to turn on the light'. To describe an event in terms of its cause is not to identify the event with its cause, nor does explanation by redescription exclude causal explanation.

The example serves also to refute the claim that we cannot describe the action without using words that link it to the alleged cause. Here the action is to be explained under the description: 'my flipping the switch', and the alleged cause is 'my wanting to turn on the light'. What possible logical relation is supposed to hold between these phrases? It seems more plausible to urge a logical link between 'my turning on the light' and 'my wanting to turn on the light', but even here the link turned out, on inspection, to be grammatical rather than logical.

In any case there is something very odd in the idea that causal

---

[1]This argument can be found, in one or more versions, in Kenny, Hampshire, and Melden, as well as in P. Winch, *The Idea of a Social Science*, London, 1958, and R. S. Peters, *The Concept of Motivation*, London, 1958. In one of its forms, the argument was of course inspired by Ryle's treatment of motives in *The Concept of Mind*.

relations are empirical rather than logical. What can this mean? Surely not that every true causal statement is empirical. For suppose '*A* caused *B*' is true. Then the cause of *B* = *A*; so, substituting, we have 'The cause of *B* caused *B*', which is analytic. The truth of a causal statement depends on *what* events are described; its status as analytic or synthetic depends on *how* the events are described. Still, it may be maintained that a reason rationalizes an action only when the descriptions are appropriately fixed, and the appropriate descriptions are not logically independent.

Suppose that to say a man wanted to turn on the light *meant* that he would perform any action he believed would accomplish his end. Then the statement of his primary reason for flipping the switch would entail that he flipped the switch—'straightway he acts,' as Aristotle says. In this case there would certainly be a logical connexion between reason and action, the same sort of connexion as that between 'It's water-soluble and was placed in water' and 'It dissolved'. Since the implication runs from description of cause to description of effect but not conversely, naming the cause still gives information. And, though the point is often overlooked, 'Placing it in water caused it to dissolve' does not entail 'It's water-soluble'; so the latter has additional explanatory force. Nevertheless, the explanation would be far more interesting if, in place of solubility, with its obvious definitional connexion with the event to be explained, we could refer to some property, say a particular crystalline structure, whose connexion with dissolution in water was known only through experiment. Now it is clear why primary reasons like desires and wants do not explain actions in the relatively trivial way solubility explains dissolvings. Solubility, we are assuming, is a pure disposition property: it is defined in terms of a single test. But desires cannot be defined in terms of the actions they may rationalize, even though the relation between desire and action is not simply empirical; there are other, equally essential criteria for desires—their expression in feelings and in actions that they do not rationalize, for example. The person who has a desire (or want or belief) does not normally need criteria at all—he generally knows, even in the absence of any clues available to others, what he wants, desires, and believes. These logical features of primary reasons show that it is not just lack of ingenuity that keeps us from defining them as dispositions to act for these reasons.

C. According to Hume, 'we may define a cause to be an object, followed by another, and where all the objects similar to the first are followed by objects similar to the second'. But, Hart and Honoré claim, 'The statement that one person did something because, for example, another threatened him, carries no implication or covert assertion that if the circumstances were repeated the same action would follow' (52). Hart and Honoré allow that Hume is right in saying that ordinary singular causal statements imply generalizations, but wrong for this very reason in supposing that motives and desires are ordinary causes of actions. In brief, laws are involved essentially in ordinary causal explanations, but not in rationalizations.

It is common to try to meet this argument by suggesting that we do have rough laws connecting reasons and actions, and these can, in theory, be improved. True, threatened people do not always respond in the same way; but we may distinguish between threats and also between agents, in terms of their beliefs and attitudes.

The suggestion is delusive, however, because generalizations connecting reasons and actions are not—and cannot be sharpened into—the kind of law on the basis of which accurate predictions can reliably be made. If we reflect on the way in which reasons determine choice, decision, and behaviour, it is easy to see why this is so. What emerges, in the *ex post facto* atmosphere of explanation and justification, as *the* reason frequently was, to the agent at the time of action, one consideration among many, *a* reason. Any serious theory for predicting action on the basis of reasons must find a way of evaluating the relative force of various desires and beliefs in the matrix of decision; it cannot take as its starting point the refinement of what is to be expected from a single desire. The practical syllogism exhausts its role in displaying an action as falling under one reason; so it cannot be subtilized into a reconstruction of practical reasoning, which involves the weighing of competing reasons. The practical syllogism provides a model neither for a predictive science of action nor for a normative account of evaluative reasoning.

Ignorance of competent predictive laws does not inhibit valid causal explanation, or few causal explanations could be made. I am certain the window broke because it was struck by a rock—I saw it all happen; but I am not (is anyone?) in command of laws on the basis of which I can predict what blows will break which windows. A generalization like 'Windows are fragile, and fragile things tend to break when struck hard enough, other conditions being right' is not a predictive law in the rough—the predictive law, if we had it, would be quantitative and would use very different concepts. The generalization, like our generalizations about behaviour, serves a different function: it provides evidence for the existence of a causal law covering the case at hand.

We are usually far more certain of a singular causal connexion than we are of any causal law governing the case; does this show that Hume was wrong in claiming that singular causal statements entail laws? Not necessarily, for Hume's claim, as quoted above, is ambiguous. It may mean that '*A* caused *B*' entails some particular law involving the predicates used in the descriptions '*A*' and '*B*', or it may mean that '*A* caused *B*' entails that there exists a causal law instantiated by some true descriptions of *A* and *B*.[1] Obviously, both versions of Hume's doctrine give a sense to the claim that singular causal statements entail laws, and both sustain the view that causal explanations 'involve laws.' But the second version is far weaker, in that no particular law is entailed by a singular causal claim, and a singular causal claim can be defended, if it needs defence, without defending any law. Only the second version of Hume's doctrine can be made to fit with most causal explanations; it suits rationalizations equally well.

The most primitive explanation of an event gives its cause; more elaborate explanations may tell more of the story, or defend the singular causal claim by producing a relevant law or by giving reasons for believing such exists. But it is an error to think no explanation has been given until a law has been produced. Linked with these errors is the idea that singular causal statements necessarily indicate, by the concepts they employ, the concepts that will occur in the entailed law. Suppose a hurricane, which is reported on page 5 of Tuesday's *Times*, causes a catastrophe, which is reported on page 13 of Wednesday's *Tribune*. Then the event reported on page 5 of Tuesday's *Times* caused the event reported on page 13 of Wednesday's *Tribune*. Should we look for a law relating events of these *kinds*? It is only slightly less ridiculous to look for a law relating hurricanes and catastrophes. The laws needed to predict the catastrophe with precision would, of course, have no use for concepts like hurricane and catastrophe. The trouble with predicting the weather is that the

---

[1] We could roughly characterize the analysis of singular causal statements hinted at here as follows: '*A* caused *B*' is true if and only if there are descriptions of *A* and *B* such that the sentence obtained by putting these descriptions for '*A*' and '*B*' in '*A* caused *B*' follows from a true causal law. This analysis is saved from triviality by the fact that not all true generalizations are causal laws; causal laws are distinguished (though of course this is no analysis) by the fact that they are inductively confirmed by their instances and by the fact that they support counterfactual and subjunctive singular causal statements.

descriptions under which events interest us—'a cool, cloudy day with rain in the afternoon'—have only remote connexions with the concepts employed by the more precise known laws.

The laws whose existence is required if reasons are causes of actions do not, we may be sure, deal in the concepts in which rationalizations must deal. If the causes of a class of events (actions) fall in a certain class (reasons) and there is a law to back each singular causal statement, it does not follow that there is any law connecting events classified as reasons with events classified as actions—the classifications may even be neurological, chemical, or physical.

D. It is said that the kind of knowledge one has of one's own reasons in acting is not compatible with the existence of a causal relation between reasons and actions: a person knows his own intentions in acting infallibly, without induction or observation, and no ordinary causal relation can be known in this way. No doubt our knowledge of our own intentions in acting will show many of the oddities peculiar to first-person knowledge of one's own pains, beliefs, desires, and so on; the only question is whether these oddities prove that reasons do not cause, in any ordinary sense at least, the actions that they rationalize.

You may easily be wrong about the truth of a statement of the form 'I am poisoning Charles because I want to save him pain', because you may be wrong about whether you are poisoning Charles—you may yourself be drinking the poisoned cup by mistake. But it also seems that you may err about your reasons, particularly when you have two reasons for an action, one of which pleases you and one which does not. For example, you do want to save Charles pain; you also want him out of the way. You may be wrong about which motive made you do it.

The fact that you may be wrong does not show that in general it makes sense to ask you how you know what your reasons were or to ask for your evidence. Though you may, on rare occasions, accept public or private evidence as showing you are wrong about your reasons, you usually have no evidence and make no observations. Then your knowledge of your own reasons for your actions is not generally inductive, for where there is induction, there is evidence. Does this show the knowledge is not causal? I cannot see that it does.

Causal laws differ from true but nonlawlike generalizations in that their instances confirm them; induction is, therefore, certainly a good way to learn the truth of a law. It does not follow that it is the only way to learn the truth of a law. In any case, in order to know that a singular causal statement is true, it is not necessary to know the truth of a law; it is necessary only to know that some law covering the events at hand exists. And it is far from evident that induction, and induction alone, yields the knowledge that a causal law satisfying certain conditions exists. Or, to put it differently, one case is often enough, as Hume admitted, to persuade us that a law exists, and this amounts to saying that we are persuaded, without direct inductive evidence, that a causal relation exists.[1]

E. Finally I should like to say something about a certain uneasiness some philosophers feel in speaking of causes of actions at all. Melden, for example, says that actions are often identical with bodily movements, and that bodily movements have causes; yet he denies that the causes are causes of the actions. This is, I think, a contradiction. He is led to it by the following sort of consideration: 'It is futile to attempt to explain conduct through the causal efficacy of desire—all *that* can explain is further happenings, not actions performed by agents. The agent confronting the causal nexus in which such happenings occur is a helpless victim of all that occurs in and to him' (128, 129). Unless I am mistaken, this argument, if it were valid, would show that actions cannot have causes at all. I shall not point out the obvious difficulties in removing actions from the realm of causality entirely. But perhaps it is worth trying to uncover the source of the trouble. Why on earth should a cause turn an action into a mere happening and a person into a helpless victim? Is it because we tend to assume, at least in the arena of action, that a cause demands a causer, agency an agent? So we press the question; if my action is caused, what caused it? If I did, then there is the absurdity of infinite regress; if I did not, I am a victim. But of course the alternatives are not exhaustive. Some causes have no agents. Primary among these are those states and changes of state in persons which, because they are reasons as well as causes, make persons voluntary agents.

[1] My thinking on the subject of this section, as on most of the topics discussed in this paper, has been greatly influenced by years of talk with Professor Daniel Bennett, now of Brandeis University.

VI

ACTION AND RESPONSIBILITY

Joel Feinberg

WHAT is the difference between a full-fledged human action and a mere bodily movement? Discussion of this ancient question, long at an impasse, was revitalized a decade and a half ago by H. L. A. Hart's classic article on the subject,[1] in which he argued that the primary function of action sentences is to ascribe responsibility, and that even in non-legal discourse such sentences are 'defeasible' in the manner of certain legal claims and judgements. It is now widely agreed, I think, that Professor Hart's analysis, while containing insights of permanent importance, still falls considerably short of the claims its author originally made for it. Yet, characteristically, there appears to be very little agreement over which features of the analysis are 'insights' and which 'mistakes'. I shall, accordingly, attempt to isolate and give some nourishment to what I take to be the kernel of truth in Hart's analysis, while avoiding, as best I can, his errors. I shall begin with that class of action sentences for which Hart's analysis has the greatest prima facie plausibility—those attributing to their subjects various kinds of substandard performance.

I. FAULTY-ACTION SENTENCES AND DEFEASIBILITY[2]

If I throw down my cards at the end of a hand of poker and, with anger in my voice, say to another player, 'You kept an ace up your sleeve!', or more simply, 'You cheated!', then surely I am doing more than 'describing his bodily movements'; I am *charging* him with an offence, *accusing* him of a wrong. It is at least plausible to interpret

From *Philosophy in America*, ed. M. Black (Allen & Unwin, 1965), pp. 134–60. Reprinted by permission of the author and George Allen and Unwin Ltd.

[1] H. L. A. Hart, 'The Ascription of Responsibility and Rights', *Proceedings of the Aristotelian Society*, Vol. 49 (1948–49), pp. 171–94.

[2] I am grateful to my colleague George Pitcher for pointing out some serious errors in an earlier version of this section. I fear there may still be much in it that he disagrees with.

utterances of that sort as claims that a person is deserving of censure or punishment for what he did. But though charges of deceit, cruelty, and the like are no doubt the most dramatic examples of pronouncements ascribing sub-par performance, it would probably be a mistake to consider them to the exclusion of other no less 'typical' ascriptions of defective behaviour. While 'condemnatory verbs'[1] such as 'cheat' and 'murder' are of course used to impute faulty actions, they are not the only verbs to do so. Such words as 'miscalculate' and 'stammer' also have faultiness built into their meaning. Miscalculating is a faulty way of calculating, and stammering is a defective way of speaking; and yet miscalculators and stammerers are not (necessarily) deserving of censure or punishment. Similarly, we speak of failing tests and muffing lines, of bumbling, botching, breaking, and spoiling—all defective ways of acting, but none necessarily morally defective.

Let us turn now to that feature of legal language which Hart called 'defeasibility', with the aim of discovering how (and to what extent) it applies to 'faulty-action sentences' interpreted in this broad way. Hart borrowed the term 'defeasible' from the law of property, where it is used to refer to an estate or legal interest in land which is 'subject to termination or "defeat" in a number of different contingencies but remains intact if no such contingencies mature'.[2] He then extended its meaning to cover all legal claims that are regarded as provisionally established at a certain stage of the litigation process but still vulnerable to defeat, annulment, or revocation at some later stage of the proceedings. Defeasibility then, if I understand Hart's intentions, is closely associated with the legal notion of a prima facie case: 'A litigating party is said to have a prima facie case when the evidence in his favour is sufficiently strong for his opponent to be called upon to answer it. A prima facie case, then, is one which is established by sufficient evidence, and can be overthrown only by rebutting evidence adduced on the other side.'[3] If a plaintiff in a civil action fails to state a claim that, if established, would amount to a prima facie case, then there is nothing against which the defendant need defend himself and he wins a directed verdict. If the plaintiff does state a claim that, if established, would amount to a prima facie case,

[1] The term is Pitcher's. See his penetrating article 'Hart on Action and Responsibility', *Philosophical Review*, Vol. 69 (1960), pp. 226–35.

[2] Hart, op. cit., p. 175.

[3] Black's *Law Dictionary*, Fourth Edition, p. 1353.

then there are a variety of defensive postures open to a defendant. He might deny some of the plaintiff's factual allegations, he might argue that the court lacks jurisdiction, or he might make an 'affirmative defence', that is, in effect, provisionally grant the plaintiff's prima facie case, but put forward some one or more of a variety of justifications, excuses, or claimed immunities. The burden of proof switches at this point from plaintiff to defendant, and this is just one of several procedural consequences of the distinction between prima facie case and affirmative defence. In a criminal grand jury trial, the *only* question before the court is whether or not there is evidence tending to establish a prima facie case against the accused, hence the jury need not even hear the evidence for the defence.

The notion of defeasibility then is inextricably tied up with an adversary system of litigation and its complex and diverse rules governing the sufficiency and insufficiency of legal claims, presumptive and conclusive evidence, the roles of contending parties, and the burden of proof. Of course there are no rules of comparable complexity and precision governing our everyday nontechnical use of 'faulty-action sentences'. At most, then, the assertion that these everyday ascriptions are defeasible suggests only that there are revealing analogies between them and legal claims in respect to their presumptiveness and vulnerability. In particular, I think, Hart would emphasize the vulnerability of both to defeat by excuses (for example, accident, mistake) and justifications (for example, forced choice of the lesser evil, special privilege, consent) but not by such other affirmative defences as diplomatic immunity, expiration of the statute of limitations, and so on. The point is that given certain rules of courtroom procedure, various types of excuse and justification are among those defences which can defeat legal claims and charges even when all the other conditions necessary and normally sufficient for their success (the 'prima facie case') are satisfied. But in everyday life outside of courtrooms there is rarely a conception of 'prima facie case' at all comparable in definiteness to the legal model (after all, in the law what is to be included in a prima facie case is largely determined by administrative convenience and other considerations having no counterpart in private life); hence outside of the law the notion of 'necessary and normally sufficient conditions' will be necessarily vague, though not necessarily obscure.

Of the several different kinds of nonlegal fault-imputations, the most persuasive examples of defeasibility are those ascribing intentional wrongdoing. When we catch a poker player with an ace up his sleeve, we have established a powerful presumption ('prima facie case') that he has *cheated*. Now it is up to him to give a satisfactory explanation (he has the 'burden of proof'), and unless he rebuts the presumption (offers an acceptable excuse), the charge will stick. The word 'cheat' is, in fact, an especially clear case, for its character as defeasible by excuses seems part of its very meaning. This is shown by the obvious absurdity of such phrases as 'unintentional cheating' and 'accidental cheating'. (Compare 'accidental murder', 'unintentional lie'.) If the 'defeating' excuse is accepted, the fault-imputation *must* be withdrawn; this is what it means for a fault-imputation to be defeasible, and it allows us to show that 'cheat', 'murder', and 'lie' are defeasible faults. I have widened the notion of 'fault-imputation' to include faults of all kinds. Are all fault-imputations then equally defeasible?

It is of considerable philosophical importance, I think, especially for consideration of the free-will problem, to realize that some faults are defeasible while some are not. Consider first of all the faults or defects we might impute to objects other than persons. Flatness is surely a 'fault' in an automobile tyre and rottenness in an egg. When we attribute such defects to tyres and eggs, we leave no space for the reply, 'But that tyre has travelled 50,000 miles and that egg was put in an inefficient refrigerator; therefore you are being too severe to call them flat and rotten respectively'. Ready analogues are found in human beings. Faulty posture (deformity), faulty health (sickness), faulty appearance (ugliness), faulty intelligence (stupidity), and faulty knowledge (ignorance) seem equally clear examples of non-defeasible faults. When we come to faulty character the situation is more difficult. Tactlessness, humourlessness, social obtuseness, are, I think, character faults that are non-defeasible. Of course, we can often explain why a man is tactless, for example, but no explanation in this case will explain away the fact once its normal sufficient conditions have been ascertained to hold; and this is precisely the mark of a non-defeasible fault: it can be explained, but not 'explained away'. Something like defective vision is at the root of these character flaws, and social or moral blindness, like its physical counterpart, can be rued or forgiven or deplored when it clearly shows itself, but not denied.

Other character faults, however, do seem clearly to be defeasible. Perhaps the clearest cases are the highly determinable or generic faults—'wickedness', for example. Any number of defences—mistaken beliefs, defective glands, neurotic compulsion, etc.—will defeat this imputation utterly. Less certain but still probable examples are such flaws as laziness and cruelty. If an apparently normal man is observed spending day after day sleeping until noon, lolling about his rooms, and engaging in only trivial and undemanding activities, there is a presumption that he is lazy. The presumption is not conclusive, however, but only defeasible, as we would soon admit if we learned that he was behaving in an apparently indolent way only because his physician had ordered him to do so, and that he was restless, bored, and impatient to resume an active life. That laziness is defeasible is indicated by the absurdity of such a phrase as 'unintentional' or 'unwilling laziness'. The absurdity is only partly accounted for (if at all) by the fact that laziness is by and large a dispositional word, for it would be equally absurd to say of a man that he spent an hour or a day being unwillingly or unwittingly lazy. The words simply do not go together even when 'lazy' bears an occurrent sense. Similarly, the man who is disposed to act regularly in a way which causes a certain class of people pain may only seem cruel, and the appearance will be a deception if in fact he acts that way because he believes he thereby causes those persons pleasure. Mistaken beliefs usually defeat the charge of cruelty (both cruel habits and cruel acts) as is evidenced by the oddness of the phrase 'unknowing cruelty'. 'Cruelty', however, is typical of a class of fault-words that have evolved or are evolving senses in which they stand for the sort of behaviour normally associated with the fault in the primary (defeasible) sense, even when in fact disassociated from that fault. So, for example, it *can* make sense, in some contexts, to speak of a kind man's (unknowingly) cruel behaviour, although even in these sense-giving contexts, the faintest odour of paradox lingers in the air.

Our main interest here, however, is not with faulty character but with faulty performance, not with fault-imputing nouns and adjectives but with faulty-action verbs. Here again it is possible to find clear examples of both defeasible and non-defeasible imputations. 'He broke the window' and 'He broke down and cried' seem to be non-defeasible, while their distant relative 'He broke faith with his friend' seems defeasible. A man who accidentally breaks a window nevertheless breaks the window. We may forgive him because his faulty performance was accidental, but for all that we do not withdraw the fault-imputing verb or 'defeat' its imputation. He broke down and cried *understandably* perhaps, but the explanation does not cancel the fact of the breakdown. Breaking faith, however, is a fish from another kettle. One cannot break faith unintentionally; for if what one did was done by mistake or accident it cannot properly be called 'breaking faith'. We should have to withdraw the charge of faithbreaking altogether once we acknowledge the excuse. Faithbreaking, in short, is defeasible. Other examples of *non-defeasible* charges of faulty performance are: 'He drove dangerously', 'He dropped the ball' (in a baseball game), 'He spoke falsely'. But 'He drove recklessly', 'He fumbled the ball' (in baseball), 'He lied', are all *defeasible*. All alike are ascriptions of performances that are in some way faulty or defective; but some we would withdraw if the subject had a proper excuse, while the others we cannot withdraw so long as we admit that conditions 'normally sufficient' for their truth are satisfied.

What is the basis of the distinction between defeasible and non-defeasible ascriptions of faulty performance? Both kinds of ascriptions express blame, at least in the very general sense that they attribute to an agent a performance somehow defective or untoward. The distinctive feature of the defeasible ascriptions is that they express a blame *above and beyond* the mere untowardness or defectiveness of the ascribed action. Still, as we have seen, it would be much *too* strong to say that all the verbs in the defeasible ascriptions, unlike their more 'neutral' counterparts, always express moral condemnation (although it is sometimes plausible to say this of some of them). In what way then is their blame 'stronger' and 'beyond' mere ascription of fault?

There is something quasi-judicial or quasi-official about the defeasible ascriptions, I would like to suggest, even when uttered outside of institutional contexts, which helps distinguish them from the non-defeasible ones. To lie or cheat, to fail to show due care, to fumble the ball or flub one's lines, is not merely to do something untoward or defective; it is also to be 'to blame' for doing it. This in turn means that the doing of the untoward act can be *charged* to one, or *registered* for further notice, or 'placed as an entry on one's *record*'. Outside institutional contexts, of course, there are no formal records but only reputations. Perhaps that is what the notion of a 'moral record' comes to. The concept of a record, however, is primarily and originally an institutional concept. Our formal records are found in offices of employment, schools, banks, and police dossiers, and they are full of grades and averages, marks and points, merits, demerits, debits, charges, credits, and registered instances of 'fault'. These records in turn have a hundred different uses, from determining the value of a baseball player to his team to dictating decisions about whether to trust, hire, fire, reward, or punish someone. Without all these records and their informal analogue (reputation) there would be no point to talk of being 'to blame' and no need for the defeasible ascriptions of fault.

To defeat the charge of being to blame by presenting a relevant strong excuse is to demonstrate that an action's faultiness is not properly 'registrable' on one of the agent's records, not chargeable to 'his account'. The reason why a faulty action is sometimes not chargeable to an agent's record even though the action was, under another description, his, is that it was performed under such circumstances that to enter it on the relevant record would make it misleading, and thus defeat its point or purpose. In a baseball game, for example, a fielder is normally said to have fumbled a ball when he is able to get his glove on it without having to run very far and yet is unable to hold on to it once he touches it. If the ball, however, strikes a pebble and takes a bad hop before striking the fielder's glove, the fielder is not then properly chargeable either with an 'error' on his official record or with having 'fumbled the ball' on his 'unofficial record' or reputation. And the reason for the acceptability of this 'strong defence' is found in the very purpose of keeping fielders' records, namely, to allow interested parties to make as accurate as possible an appraisal of the contribution of each player to the success or failure of the team.[1] If we charge fielders for the consequences of fortuitous events the records will lose their accuracy and fail accordingly to achieve their purpose. A similar account, I think, could be given the rationale of entries on other professional, legal, and even 'moral' records.

It might be argued against this sketchy account that *any* kind of fault can be put on some sort of record or other, hence 'registrability' cannot very well be the characteristic which distinguishes defeasible from non-defeasible faults. But the point I am endeavouring to make is not one about logical conceivability; it is one about practical plausibility. On what sort of record might we register that Jones drove dangerously, if it should turn out that the risk he created by driving ten miles an hour over the speed limit was amply justified by his purpose in getting a critically ill passenger to the hospital? Should we put this down as a fault on his *driving record*? Surely not, if the point of keeping a driving record is to reveal what kind of driver a man is—safe and capable or careless and dangerous. Jones drove dangerously on this occasion, to be sure, but the circumstances were so special that his behaviour did nothing to reveal his *predominant*

---

[1]This is very close to the function of 'records' in history. Cf. H. L. A. Hart and A. M. Honoré: 'History is written not only to satisfy the need for explanation, but also the desire to identify and assess contributions made by historical figures to changes of importance; to triumphs and disasters, and to human happiness or suffering.' *Causation in the Law*, Oxford 1959, p. 59.

tendencies, hence to register it as a fault would not promote the purpose of the record itself. Smith speaks falsely on a given occasion. On what imaginable record might this have a point as an entry? On his *moral record*? Surely not, unless he spoke with intent to deceive, in which case he *lied*—and that *is* registrable. In general, I should think, a person's faulty act is registrable only if it reveals what sort of person he is in some respect about which others have a practical interest in being informed.

There are at least three different types of 'registrable' (defeasible) faults, each exhibiting its own peculiarities. Depending on their purposes, record keepers might register (1) instances of defective skill or ability (for example, 'fumbles'), (2) instances of defective or improper care or effort (negligence, laziness) and (3) instances of improper intention (cheating, breaking faith). There are similarities in the uses to which these three distinct types of entries might be put—and also differences. In all three types of cases, to be forewarned is to be forearmed. If there are numerous instances of cheating on a man's record then we had better not play cards with him, or if we play we should watch him closely. Similarly, if a man's record shows him to be careless and absent-minded, then we should hire another and not him to be a night watchman; and if Butterfinger's fielding average is substantially lower than Orthodigit's, we had better install the latter at third base in the ninth inning with our team ahead in a close game.

On the other hand, corresponding to the three types of faults, there are important differences in the modes of treatment we might inflict on their possessors. We should not punish or censure the fumbler, for example, even if we were in a position to do so, except of course to make him try harder; but then the censure is for defective effort, not defective skill. However else we are to analyse punishment and censure, we must include an element of expressed disapproval, perhaps even hostility and resentment; and these attitudes and judgements, while they might intensify desire and even change intention, could have little effect (except perhaps inhibiting) on skill. Censure apparently works best in fortifying the motivation of otherwise careless, distractable, and lazy people, that is, those with faulty records of the second type. There is now apparently some reason to think that manifest hostility, warnings, and threats work less well in correcting faults of improper intention, and in respect at least to the most severe defects of this sort, are useless or self-defeating. To *express* disapproval, for example, to the man with a powerful grudge against society may simply intensify his hatred, and promote rather than hinder further hateful and destructive behaviour.

If we mean by 'blame' any sort of outwardly manifested disapproval of a person for his defective performance, then the relations between blaming and 'being to blame' are diverse and complex indeed. The defeasible fault-imputations charge only that a man is *to blame* for his defective performance (and not merely that the performance *was* defective) but not that he is properly subject to any kind of overt blame for it. Whether to blame him or not depends on what use we wish to make of his 'record', and this in turn depends upon our prior purposes, the nature of the fault, and the prospects of 'utility'.

In summary: I have distinguished three different stages in our responses to faulty performance. We can simply note that a given act is Jones's and that it was in some way faulty or defective. At this stage we need not use the language of defeasible fault-ascriptions at all. We might simply say, for instance, that he dropped the ball, departed from the blueprints, spoke falsely, etc. At a second stage, we might resort to the language of defeasible ascriptions and charge him, for example, with fumbling the ball, botching the job, or lying. At this stage we not only ascribe to him an action which is somehow defective, we also hold him *to blame* for it. This involves registering the defective performance on the agent's relevant record, or in the absence of a formal record and an institutional context, making it part of his reputation. At the third stage, we may put the record or reputation, with the fault duly registered therein, to any one of a great variety of *uses*, including, among other things, overt blame. If we think, on the basis of the record, that overt blame is what the agent deserves, we might say that he is properly subject to—or liable to—blame, and then that judgement could be characterized as an *ascription of liability*. But being 'to blame' and being subject to further blaming performances are two quite distinct things: the former is often a necessary but only rarely a sufficient condition for the latter.

We shall stop at the first stage (non-defeasible fault-ascription) if an appropriate defence defeats the charge that the defect is registrable; or we may stop at the second stage (register that the agent is 'to blame' for the fault) if there is no reason to expect any kind of overt responsive action toward the agent to achieve anything useful. Finally, we may think it necessary to blame or fire or punish him, in which case we hold him (now at the third stage) so liable. In respect to the normal non-faulty action, however, we do not even get to the first stage.

II. NORMAL-ACTION SENTENCES

Can we conclude by accepting this complicated version of Hart's analysis as holding good for faulty-action sentences only? Was Hart simply misled, as some critics[1] have charged, by his own unrepresentative selection of examples, oddly failing to notice the difference between such accusations as 'He murdered her' (and 'He fumbled the ball') on the one hand, and such normal, nonaccusing sentences as 'He closed the door' on the other? This is a tidy way of disposing of Hart's view, but I suspect that it does less than full justice to his insight. Hart must surely have intended, and perhaps with good reason, that the notions of ascriptiveness and defeasibility throw some light on the normal cases of action as well as on defective performance. This is the critical possibility that will be explored in the remainder of this paper.

Is there any sense in which normal-action sentences ascribe responsibility? If we consider the matter closely, we shall discover at least five closely related but distinguishable things that might be meant by the phrase 'ascription of responsibility'.

(1) *Straightforward Ascriptions of Causality*

A meteorologist might ascribe today's weather in New England to yesterday's pressure system over the Great Lakes, meaning simply that the latter is the cause of the former. In similar ways we frequently ascribe causality not only to the presence or absence of impersonal events, states, and properties, but also to the actions, omissions, properties, and dispositions of human beings. Ascriptions of causality, whether to impersonal or to personal sources, often use the language of responsibility. A low pressure system over the Great Lakes, we might naturally say, was *responsible* for the storms in New England; and in precisely the same (causal) sense we might say that a man's action was responsible for some subsequent event or state of affairs, imputing no more blame or credit or guilt or liability to the man than we do to the pressure system when we ascribe causality to it. When we say then that Smith is responsible for X we can mean simply that X is the result of what Smith did or, in equivalent terms, that Smith did something (e.g. turned the knob) and thereby caused X (e.g. the door's opening) to happen.

Gilbert Ryle has argued that we do not speak of persons as respon-

---

[1] E.g. Pitcher, op. cit., and P. T. Geach, 'Ascriptivism', *Philosophical Review*, Vol. 69 (1960), p. 221.

sible for states of affairs unless we are charging them with some sort of offence.[1] There is a point overstated in this claim, but not one which militates against a purely causal sense of 'responsible'. The point is this: we do not ordinarily raise the question of responsibility for something unless that something has somehow excited our interest, and as a matter of fact the states of affairs that excite our interest are very often unhappy ones. But sometimes unexpectedly happy circumstances need accounting for too, and sometimes the interest aroused is the desire to understand, not the desire to give credit or blame. The language of responsibility aside, we do not usually raise the question of the *causation* of something, either, unless that something has somehow excited our interest. The things that cry out for explanation are usually those that first appear somehow 'fishy'; but as Stanley Cavell points out, they need not be 'morally fishy'.[2]

(2) *Ascriptions of Causal-Agency*

To characterize these properly, we must introduce a rough distinction between complex and simple acts. There are a great number of ways in which actions are complex, but only one of these concerns us here, that which might be called 'causal complexity'. To accomplish such tasks as moving one's furniture to a warehouse or rescuing a drowning swimmer, one must first take a number of other steps, such as lifting chairs, diving into the water, etc. The complex task is performed by means of the performance of a series of teleologically connected 'sub-acts': one closes a door *by* pushing and latching it.

A causally simple case of doing, on the other hand, requires no earlier doing as a means. Smiling and frowning are simple actions, and so are raising one's arm and shutting one's eyes. To do any of these things it is not first necessary to do something else; nor is it necessary to do something in one's mind as a kind of triggering: to set off a volition or 'flex an occult non-muscle'.[3] In very special circumstances, of course, these normally simple acts can be complex. I might have to make myself smile, for social purposes, by a kind of interior girding of my tired facial muscles;[4] but normally one smiles spontaneously without having to 'cause' himself to do so.

[1]Gilbert Ryle, *The Concept of Mind*, New York 1949, p. 69.

[2]Stanley Cavell, 'Must We Mean What We Say?', *Inquiry*, Vol. 1 (1958), p. 177.

[3]Ryle, op. cit., p. 74: 'To frown intentionally is not to bring about a frown-causing exertion of some occult non-muscle.'

[4]Cf. Ralph Waldo Emerson: 'There is a mortifying experience . . . I mean "the foolish face of praise", the forced smile we put on in company where we do not

Any distinction in terms of simplicity and complexity is, of course, a matter of degree. Winking and smiling are usually perfectly simple actions; grasping, clutching, throwing only slightly more complex; baking a cake, or building a house more complex still. Some relatively complex actions, such as walking, rising, and sitting down, do not involve in their bare descriptions any explicit reference to an external object transformed or manipulated. These can be distinguished from those complex actions typically referred to by transitive verbs, such as 'open', 'close', 'rescue', 'kill', with their objects. Only the latter are referred to here by the phrase 'causally complex actions'.

Now in respect of causally connected sequences of acts and consequences, our language provides us with numerous alternative ways of talking. J. L. Austin describes one of these options: '. . . a single term descriptive of what he did may be made to cover either a smaller or a larger stretch of events, those excluded by the narrower description being then called "consequences" or "results" or "effects" or the like of his act'.[1] Thus we can say that Jones opened the door and thereby caused Smith (who was inside) to be startled, in this way treating Jones's act as the cause of a subsequent effect; or we can say (simply) 'Jones startled Smith' (by opening the door), and thus incorporate the consequence into the complex action. If Smith suffered a heart attack and died, we can say that Jones's opening the door caused his death, or that Jones's startling him caused his death, or simply that Jones killed him (by doing those things).

This well-known feature of our language, whereby a man's action can be described as narrowly or broadly as we please, I propose to call the 'accordion effect', because an act, like the folding musical instrument, can be squeezed down to a minimum or else stretched out. He turned the key, he opened the door, he startled Smith, he killed Smith—all of these are things we might say that Jones *did* with one identical set of bodily movements. Because of the accordion effect we can usually replace any ascription to a person of causal responsibility by an ascription of agency or authorship. We can, if we wish, puff out an action to include an effect, and more often than not our language obliges us by providing a relatively complex action word for the purpose. Instead of saying Smith did *A* (a relatively simple act) and

feel at ease, in answer to conversation which does not interest us. The muscles, not spontaneously moved but moved by a low usurping wilfulness, grow tight about the outline of the face, with the most disagreeable sensation', *Essays, First Series,* Boston 1895, pp. 56–57.

[1] J. L. Austin, 'A Plea for Excuses', *Philosophical Papers*, Oxford 1961, p. 149.

thereby caused X in Y, we might say something of the form 'Smith X-ed Y'; instead of 'Smith opened the door causing Jones to be startled', 'Smith startled Jones'.

Ascriptions of causal responsibility, then, are often precisely equivalent to ascriptions of the second type, which we have called ascriptions of causal agency. Whatever difference exists between the two forms of expression is merely a matter of rhetorical emphasis or grammatical convenience.[1] Both say something about causation, the one quite explicitly, the other in the language of agency or authorship.

(3) *Ascriptions of Simple Agency*

These cannot possibly be assimilated to the first two. The purely causal ascriptions can usually be translated into ascriptions of causal-agency, and the latter of course can only be of causally complex actions. Simple actions (as is now widely acknowledged) have no causal component. In order to open a door, we must first do something else which will *cause* the door to open; but to move one's finger one simply moves it—no prior causal activity is required. Hence ascriptions of simple agency are ascriptions of agency through and through. One cannot play the accordion with them.

(4) *Imputations of Fault*

This motley group, discussed in Part I, have, amidst their many dissimilarities, several important features in common. All of them ascribe agency, simple or (more commonly) causal, for a somehow defective or faulty action. Many of them, but not all, are defeasible. Rather than be qualified in certain ways, these will be withdrawn altogether and replaced with non-defeasible faulty-act ascriptions. If they cannot be so 'defeated', however, they are properly entered on a relevant record of the agent's; that is, they are *registrable*. As registered faults, they are *non-transferable*. In the relevant sense of 'being to blame', no one is to blame but the agent; hence no one else can 'take the blame' (or 'shoulder the responsibility') for him.

(5) *Ascriptions of Liability*

These are different in kind from the fault-imputations, even though they are often intertwined or confused with them. The one kind imputes a faulty act, simple or complex, to an agent as its author; the other ascribes, either to the agent or to someone else, liability

---

[1]Cf. John Salmond: 'The distinction between an act and its consequences, between doing a thing and causing a thing, is a merely verbal one.' *Jurisprudence*, Eleventh edition, London 1957, p. 402.

under a set of rules or customs to some further response for it. Unlike imputations of fault, ascriptions of liability can be transferable, vicarious, or 'strict', that is, independent of actual fault. In some situations under some rules, a faultless spectator may effectively say 'I'll take the responsibility for that', or 'Charge that to my account', and the liability really does transfer as a result.

There are several morals to be drawn immediately from this fivefold classification. First of all, all five types of ascription can be made in the language of responsibility. Sometimes 'responsibility' *means* causal assignability, sometimes authorship, causal or simple, sometimes fault-imputability or creditability, sometimes liability. Often ascriptions of responsibility blend authorship and liability, these being intimately related in virtue of the fact that the most usual (though not the only) reason for holding a person liable for an action (or event) is that he performed (or caused) it. Another thing to notice about the classification is that the first three uses of 'responsible', in ascriptions of straightforward causality, causal agency, and simple agency, apply to the 'normal case' of action, where questions of fault, desert of punishment, and the like, do not arise. Quite clearly, action sentences *do* ascribe responsibility in these senses.

The classification also suggests what it means to say that a sentence *ascribes* responsibility, in any of the senses of 'responsibility'. It was very important to Hart in his original article to argue that action sentences are typically 'ascriptive' rather than 'descriptive'. But this is a confusion. Any kind of action sentence can be *used* either descriptively or ascriptively. We describe a person's actions when we have been considering that person and wondering what he did—when the question before our minds is not 'Who did it?' but rather 'What did *he* do?' When we have occasion to ascribe an action to a person, we have the action, so to speak, in our hands, and we want to know what to do with it, whom to pin it on.

If we wish to know who killed Cock Robin, this must be because we know that *someone* killed Cock Robin, but we don't know *who*. In the case of complex actions this sort of curiosity is common, for we can often examine the effects of an action in separation from the action itself and then wonder to whom to ascribe the consequence. A perfectly simple action, however, has no detachable part to examine in leisurely abstraction from the rest. Except for the simple act itself there is no further 'ascriptum' to ascribe. The statement 'Jones smiled', when it appears routinely in a novelist's narrative or a newspaper article, simply describes or reports what Jones did at a certain moment. In these cases the novelist or journalist has not *assigned* a smile to Jones, as if he had the smile first and then selected Jones to put it on.

Still, rare as they might be, there are occasions for ascribing simple acts. A simple-action sentence is used ascriptively only when a question of personal identity has, for one reason or another, arisen. 'Who was that man who smiled?' one might ask, and another might chime in 'Oh, did someone smile? Who was it?' Now the stage is set for an ascription. An ascription of simple action is about an identification of the doer of an already known doing.

Some philosophers have argued that it is an 'improper way of talking' to speak, after the fact, of a person's being responsible *for his own actions*, that strictly speaking what a person can be held responsible for are the 'consequences, results, or upshots of the things he does'.[1] This is quite true if we mean by 'responsible', *causally* responsible; for with rare exceptions we don't cause our actions, we simply do them. It would be extraordinary however if such a wide-spread idiom as 'responsibility for one's actions' always embodied such a crude mistake, and our classification reveals several 'proper' uses to which it might be put. First of all, to be responsible for one's own complex actions (e.g. closing a door) is properly to have one's simpler actions identified as the cause of an upshot. The knife cuts both ways: If 'being responsible for the door's being shut (by having caused it to close)' is a permissible way of speaking, then so is talk of being responsible *for closing* the door, which in virtue of the accordion effect is strictly equivalent to it. Secondly, to be responsible for one's simple actions is only to be properly identifiable as their doer. 'It was Mary who smiled' ascribes the responsibility *for smiling* to Mary, and says nothing whatever about causal upshots. This is especially clear when the simple action is faulty, as for example, a socially inappropriate smirk or leer. The report that someone had smiled in church, if it were to have received currency in colonial Massachusetts where such simple activity was a crime, would have set the stage for a non-causal responsibility ascription. To say then that it was Mary who did it would be to ascribe responsibility to Mary *for smiling*, not in the sense of doing something to cause the smile to appear, but rather in the sense of being properly identifiable as the doer of the deed.

[1]Pitcher, op. cit., p. 227.

III. THE STRONGER SENSE OF 'ASCRIPTIVE'

The fivefold classification of responsibility ascriptions, then, does tend to support Hart's view that action-sentences are ascriptive. It suggests at least that, for all kinds of action-sentences, there is some context in which they can be used ascriptively, that is to identify the 'author'. On the other hand it does nothing to support his view that all action-sentences ascribe *liability* to formal responses from others or that they are all defeasible in the manner of legal changes and accusations. In this section the classification will be used to restore still more of Hart's view, though perhaps not in the way he intended it to be understood.

We have already noticed one way in which the puzzling term 'ascription' can be understood. Ascriptions in this sense have a necessary subjective condition or contextual presupposition. What is not an ascription in one context may well be so in another, depending on the concerns of the speaker. If the question is 'What did Jones do?' then the sentence 'Jones did *A*' *describes* what Jones did; but if the question is 'Who did *A*?', then 'Jones did *A*' *ascribes A* to Jones. This simple distinction may seem to have very little importance, since ascriptions and descriptions, so understood, may say the same thing about a man with only different emphases provided by our interests. The distinction between ascriptions and descriptions, however, sometimes reverberates with deeper overtones. Instead of a mere matter of emphasis, the distinction is taken to be one of type. P. T. Geach,[1] for example, in criticizing Hart, compares the distinction between descriptive and ascriptive with the better known contrast between descriptive and *pre*scriptive as if they were distinctions of the same order; and K. W. Rankin contrasts 'matters of ascription' with 'matters of fact'.[2] Now whether the sentence 'Jones did *A*' is used to ascribe *A* to Jones or to describe what Jones did, as we have understood those terms, it surely registers, in either case, a matter of fact. The indicative mood is well suited to express what the sentence does in either use; and ascriptions as well as descriptions can be true or false, and are 'about' what happened. If ascriptions are to be contrasted, then, with 'matters of fact', some new conception of 'ascriptiveness' is involved. The question to be considered now is whether, in this new sense of ascription, there is any reason for treating action-sentences as ascriptive.

[1] Geach, op. cit., p. 221.

[2] K. W. Rankin, *Choice and Chance*, Oxford 1960, p. 29 *et passim*.

The stronger notion of ascriptiveness can be explained, I think, in the following way. There is a familiar commonsense distinction between questions calling for *decisions* and those requiring *discoveries*. I must decide at which restaurant to dine tomorrow, but I must discover the solution of an equation, or the population of a town. In the first case, even when all the facts are in, I have a certain amount of discretion; in the latter case, I am bound or committed totally by the facts—I cannot escape the conclusions they dictate. This distinction has been expressed in a great variety of ways: questions of policy versus questions of fact, practical versus theoretical, regulative versus constitutive, and so on. Some philosophers have denied either the existence or the importance of the distinction: 'Platonists' tend to reduce questions of decision to questions of discovery, and 'Pragmatists' assimilate the theoretical to the practical. Common sense, however, holds firm to the distinction, even when puzzled about how to explain it or where to draw the line. Philosophers who contrast 'ascriptive' with 'factual', I suggest, have this distinction in mind. By 'ascriptive sentences' they mean (among other things) sentences not *wholly* theoretical or factual, having an irreducibly discretionary aspect.

A second characteristic of ascriptions, closely connected with the first, is what may be called their 'contextual relativity'. We may have an option of ascribing X to either A, B, or C. To which of these X is properly ascribable may depend on numerous factors other than the relevant characteristics of A, B, C. Our decision may turn on our own degree of knowledge or ignorance, on our practical purposes, on the type of ascription or the nature of the 'context', on our long range policies, on institutional rules and practices, on 'values', and so on. Some of these considerations may conflict and thus call for careful weighing up—which is to say that they require not merely decision, but *judgement*. Finally, our well considered ascriptive judgements may exhibit something like what Hart calls 'defeasibility', although outside of legal and quasi-legal contexts, talk of 'cases', and 'claims', and 'defences' may not seem quite at home.

Let us now return to the fivefold classification to see what it can tell us now about 'ascriptiveness' construed as irreducibly discretionary, contextually relative, and 'something-like-defeasible'. The first thing it reveals is that ascriptions of causality, even when they do not involve persons and their actions, commonly exhibit 'ascriptiveness' construed in this fuller way. This is not to suggest that many 'causal laws' are decided upon rather than discovered, or that scientists have any 'discretion' at all in discovering and formulating laws of nature. Where scientists and others have some discretion is in a rather different sort of inquiry—when some unexplained happening has occurred, or some interesting or important state of affairs has been discovered, and we must decide to what cause to attribute it. Here, often, even after all of the facts are in, we have some choice, if what we wish to do is to *select* from the welter of causal factors that made some contribution to the event in question, one to be denominated the cause.[1]

Often the selection from among many causal candidates of 'the cause' seems so obvious that we may lose sight altogether of the fact that we are selecting, singling out, deciding. But that causal ascriptions are selective becomes clear to anyone who tries to give a *complete* causal explanation of some event in terms of all the conditions severally necessary and jointly sufficient for its occurrence. *All* of these conditions are equally important to the event, a naive person might argue, in that all were equally necessary to its occurrence. Equally important to the event perhaps, but not equally important to the investigator. The investigator talks of 'the cause' in the first place, only because he suspects that there is some single event or condition among the many causal contributors to the outcome, which it will be of special interest or importance to him or others to identify.

Which 'contributor'[2] to an event is to be labelled the cause of that event then is always a matter of selection, often an occasion for decision, even for difficult judgement, and is generally 'relative' to a variety of contextual considerations. Cataloguing the many forms of causal relativity is a large task but three might be mentioned here. First, selecting the cause of an event is relative to what is usual or normal in a given context. I. M. Copi bids us ponder the fate of the insurance investigator who reports back to his company that the cause of a mysterious fire in the house of a policy holder was 'the presence of oxygen in the air'. What the company clearly wanted him to discover was not just any necessary condition but rather 'the

---

[1] A great deal has been written in recent years about causal ascriptions. I am probably most indebted to W. Dray, *Laws and Explanation in History*, Oxford 1957; D. Gasking, 'Causation and Recipes', *Mind*, Vol. 64 (1955); N. R. Hanson, 'Causal Chains', *Mind*, Vol. 64 (1955); Hart and Honoré op. cit.; and J. L. Mackie, 'Responsibility and Language', *Australasian Journal of Philosophy*, Vol. 33 (1955).

[2] There are circumstances in which 'the cause' need not even be a necessary condition. See Hart and Honoré, op. cit., pp. 116–121. Moreover, we do not have *complete* discretion in selecting, according to our purposes and policies, the cause from the causal conditions, as Hart and Honoré have effectively and thoroughly demonstrated.

incident or action which in the presence of those conditions normally present, made the difference this time'.[1] Leaving the insurance investigator to be dealt with by his employers, we can without difficulty think of contexts where his ascription would not have raised an eyebrow. ' . . . it is easy to imagine cases', write Hart and Honoré, 'where the exclusion of oxygen would be normal, e.g. when some laboratory experiment or delicate manufacturing process depended on its exclusion for safety from fire and hence for success, and in such cases it would be correct to identify the abnormal presence of oxygen as the cause of the fire'.[2] What is 'the cause' then depends on what is 'normal', and what is normal varies with the context.

Another form of causal relativity is relativity to ignorance. Consider how we might explain to a group of workers in a welding shop how an explosion occurred in a nearby warehouse. We might say that the explosion was the result of a spark which, let us suppose, was the last conspicuous event preceding the eruption. But in a welding shop sparks are flying all the time. They are perfectly routine, and hence they can't explain anything as extraordinary as an explosion. Given the context naturally assumed by the welding shop workers, one must cite as the cause much earlier events such as the storing of TNT or leaky gasoline drums. The analogy with history, and its own brand of casual relativity, is plain. Historiographers ascribe the causes of wars, revolutions, and other such explosions, and as a rule they write for their own contemporaries. Historiographers of later ages then write of the same events but for a later group of contemporaries with a later set of conceptions of what is routine. As a result, the earlier writer ascribes 'the cause' to some political or economic equivalent of the sparks, and the later opts for some leaky oil can. One of the functions of an explanation of particular occurrences is to render them intelligible, to induce understanding of them. Intelligibility, however, is always intelligibility *to* someone, and understanding is always *someone's* understanding, and these are in part functions of what is already known or assumed to be normal or routine.

A third sort of causal relativity is relativity of practical interest. 'It is a well known fact', wrote R. B. Perry, 'that we describe as the cause of an event that particular condition by which we hope to control it.'[3] Accordingly, we tend to select as 'the cause' of an event, that

---

[1] I. M. Copi, *Introduction to Logic*, First Edition, New York 1952, p. 327.

[2] H. L. A. Hart and A. M. Honoré, 'Causation in the Law', *Law Quarterly Review*, Vol. 72 (1956), Part One, p. 75.

[3] Ralph Barton Perry, *General Theory of Value,* Cambridge, Mass. 1926, p. 394.

causal condition which—in Collingwood's felicitous metaphor—has a handle on it which we can grasp and manipulate; and thus even causal generalizations tend to function directively, or as Douglas Gasking puts it, as 'recipes' for cooking up desired effects.

The very meaning we assign the word 'cause' is likely to vary with our purposes. Those who are concerned to produce something beneficial seek 'the cause' of what they wish to produce in some new 'condition', which when conjoined with those usually present, will be *sufficient* for the desired thing to come into existence. On the other hand, those whose primary aim is to eliminate something harmful are for the most part looking for causes in the sense of *necessary condition*. That is because in order to succeed in such a task, one must find some condition in whose absence the undesirable phenomenon would not occur, and then somehow, eliminate *that* condition. Not just any necessary condition, however, will do as 'the cause'; it must be a necessary condition which technicians can get at, manipulate, modify, or destroy. Our purposes here determine what we will accept as 'the cause', and when it is the cause of an illness or a crime wave we are after, accessibility and manipulability are as important to our purposes as the 'necessity' of the condition. Indeed, we will accept as the cause of some unhappy state even some necessary condition which from the point of view of theory is obvious or trivial, provided only it *is* necessary and it is something we can get at.

It would be an oversimplification, however, to identify 'the cause' of an infelicitous condition with *any* manipulable necessary condition, no matter how trivial; and the reason this is so is that it oversimplifies not the processes of nature, but human purposes themselves. No matter how much we wish to get rid of defects and infelicities in our bodies, machines, and societies, we never wish to eliminate them at *any price*. What we want when we look for 'the cause' of unfortunate happenings is an *economical* means of eliminating them, the right 'price' being determined by our many implicit 'background purposes'.

A boozy pedestrian on a dark and rainy night steps into the path of a speeding careless motorist and is killed. What caused this regrettable accident? Since liabilities are at stake, we can expect the rival attorneys to give conflicting answers. But more than civil liability is involved. A reformer argues that the liquor laws are the cause, claiming that as long as liquor is sold in that region we can expect to have so many deaths a year. From traffic engineers, city planners, and educators we can expect still different answers;

and in a sense they might all be right, if they named genuine 'causal factors'. But that is not what their discussion is all about. Should we prevent such accidents by spending a million dollars as the traffic engineer recommends? Or fifty million as the city planner urges? Each would uproot a necessary condition, but at what expense! Perhaps the moralist is on the right track, but do we really wish to penalize thousands of innocent responsible whisky drinkers in order to prevent the deaths of a careless few? In such ways as these are interests and purposes drawn into the context of ascribing causes. They form an implicit part of every causal field determining in part the direction in which we point when we pick 'the cause' of an event.

In virtue of their discretionary character and their contextual relativity, causal ascriptions characteristically exhibit a kind of vulnerability logically analogous to the defeasibility of some legal claims and accusations. When a humanly interesting event occurs it is always possible to mention dozens of factors that have made important causal contributions to its occurrence. Even events that occurred years earlier may so qualify. (Sometimes the straw that breaks the camel's back is in the middle, or even at the bottom, of the pile.) To cite any one of these as 'the cause' is always to invite a 'rebuttal' from a partisan of one of the other 'causal candidates', just as to make an accusation is always to invite a defence; and to show in a proper way that a certain condition did make a contribution or was an indispensable condition is only to make out a presumption of causal importance which holds unless rebutted in one of the many diverse allowable ways.

In general, properly rebuttable causal ascriptions commit the error, not of misdescribing, but of representing the less important as the more important. When it is said that the presence of oxygen in the air caused the fire, or that the cause of the stomach ache was the drink of whisky (rather than an unsuspected ulcer), or that the riot was caused by the unprecedented presence of a Negro student in the dormitory, it is less to the point to call these statements false than to call them unwise, misleading, or unfair, in the manner of otherwise accurate accounts that put their emphases in the wrong places. To be sure, but for the oxygen, the drink, the presence of the Negro,[1] there would have

[1] For an account of the difficult integration of the University of Georgia, see Calvin Trillin, 'An Education in Georgia', *New Yorker*, July 13, 1963— 'On the . . . night of the riot, their [the white girls'] behaviour changed drastically. After the first brick and the first coke bottle had crashed into her room, Charlayne [Hunter] went to a partly partitioned office . . . and stayed there during most of what

been no fire, ache, or riot. However, for the purposes of our more comprehensive understanding and control of such events, other equally necessary causal factors are far more important and deserve to be mentioned first.

Given that causal ascriptions, both those that assign 'the cause' to impersonal factors and those that select out human actions, are 'ascriptive' in the stronger sense, it follows immediately, in virtue of the accordion effect, that ascriptions of causal agency are so too. If 'Jones caused the door to close' is ascriptive, then 'Jones closed the door' must be so equally. If 'causing a war by an act of assassination' is ascriptive, then the still more complex 'act' of 'starting a war' must be so too. We have found a sense, then, in which one large class of action-sentences—those attributing causal agency—are ascriptive and 'something-like-defeasible' *even when the activity in question is in no way faulty*.

Ascriptions of simple agency, however, cannot be analysed in this way, for a simple doing is not the upshot of a prior doing to which it may be ascribed, and *a fortiori* we have no discretion to *decide* whether to *select* a prior doing as 'the cause' of the simple doing in question. Whether or not a man smiled is entirely a question of fact whose answer is to be discovered, not 'decided' or 'selected' presumptively.

In so far as the word 'smile' is *vague*, of course, there is room for discretion in its application to a borderline case; but the discretion here, which is hardly peculiar to simple-action words, is of a different sort. Whether we call a borderline coloured object blue or green, we are likely to say, is a matter of indifference, or 'a mere question of words'. But when we deny that a question of causation is wholly factual, we are not contrasting 'question of fact' with 'question of language'; nor are we implying that its resolution by a decision is indifferent or arbitrary. We are implying instead that a decision cannot be made without a reference to our own practical purposes and values, which is quite another thing.

Simple-action sentences, then, such as 'Jones moved his finger', can be used ascriptively to identify an agent, but they are not ascriptive in the further strong sense that we are left with discretion to accept or reject them even after all the facts are in. Thus, in summary, Hart's critics are right in charging him with over-burdening the

followed. A group of [white] coeds soon formed a circle in front of the office and marched around, each screaming an insult as she got to the door. "They kept yelling 'Does she realize she's causing all this trouble?' " '

notion of ascriptiveness, for we have seen one class, at least, of action-sentences, the action-simples, which are not ascriptive in the sense that is opposed to 'wholly factual'. But we have restored a good part of Hart's original theory (considerably reinterpreted) that is often rejected, for we have shown that one substantial class of action-sentences that do not necessarily impute faults are nevertheless very often ascriptive in a strong sense, and that these sentences, as is shown by the characteristic ways in which they might be rebutted, are 'something-like-defeasible' as well.

IV. TWO VERSIONS OF 'THE PROBLEM OF ACTION'

How important is this restoration of a part of Hart's original thesis? That depends in large measure on one's philosophical interests and strategies. For problems of jurisprudence and moral psychology, I should think, the ascriptive and defeasible character of the action-sentences of most interest to those disciplines is a matter of great importance indeed. But for 'the problem of action' (or of 'voluntary action'), construed as a problem of metaphysics, where the concern is to distinguish activity from passivity as very general conceptual categories, the notions of ascriptiveness and defeasibility appear to be of no help whatever. It is no accident that writers in ethics and jurisprudence, when troubled by 'the problem of action', typically select as their examples more or less complex, teleologically connected sequences of behaviour that cause harm or happiness, success or failure, to self or others. They are likely to ask, for example, what distinguishes a voluntary killing from a mere accidental homicide, or a voluntary from an involuntary signing of a contract, or in general an act freely and deliberately performed from one done in circumstances that gave the agent 'no choice'. The best answer to *this* question about voluntary action, it seems to me, is that of Hart and Honoré in *Causation in the Law*: 'In common speech, and in much legal usage, a human action is said not to be voluntary or not fully voluntary if some one or more of a quite varied range of circumstances are present . . . '[1] These circumstances make a lengthy enumeration. They include, Hart and Honoré inform us,[2] physical compulsion, concussion, shock, dizziness, hypnosis; the motives of self-preservation, preservation of property, safeguarding of other rights, privileges, or interests of self or others; legal or moral obligation; unreflective,

[1] Hart and Honoré, *Causation in the Law,* p. 38.
[2] Ibid., pp. 134 ff.

instinctive, or automatic movement; mistake, accident, or even negligence. Voluntariness ('actness'?) in this sense is a matter of degree. An action done under a threat of physical violence, for example, comes closer to being fully voluntary than an act done under the threat of death. Further, voluntariness in this sense has no direct and invariant connexion with liability. An agent may be held strictly accountable for an action which is considerably 'less than fully voluntary' if the act is sufficiently harmful; and where the harm is enormously great (e.g., giving military secrets to the enemy) no degree short of complete involuntariness may relieve the agent of liability.[1]

Writers concerned with the metaphysical problem of action typically select as *their* examples such simple movements as raising one's arm or moving one's finger. When they ask what distinguishes a voluntary from an involuntary act they are inquiring about the difference between an *action* (said with emphasis) and a mere bodily movement, for example between a wink and a mere eye-twitch. Involuntariness in this sense (lack of muscular control) is only one of the circumstances that can render an act less than fully voluntary in the other sense. That is, some actions which *are* actions through and through and not automatic twitches or 'mere bodily movements' are nevertheless not fully voluntary in the sense discussed earlier because they may be done from threats or under moral obligation, etc. Now, whether an action in the sense opposed to mere bodily motion is properly to be ascribed to a person whose arm has moved is not a question that has anything to do with excuses, presumptions, and practical purposes. It has every appearance of being strictly about 'the facts', although just what kind of facts it is about is part of the metaphysical perplexity that the question naturally engenders.

On the other hand, whether or not a causally complex act is to be ascribed to a person whose relatively simple act was a causal factor in the production of some upshot depends, as we have seen, on how important a causal contribution it made, as determined by our prior assumptions and practical purposes. It is misleading to attribute '*X*-ing *Y*' to a man as his doing when other factors made more important contributions. When the action in question is 'faulty', then sometimes the 'other conditions' are mitigating *excuses* (the agent's sickness or fatigue); sometimes not—as when between the agent's act and the upshot a dozen unanticipated causal factors intervened. 'Burning

---

[1] Cf. Aristotle, *Nicomachean Ethics*, 1110^a 20–1110^b, and Hart and Honoré, op. cit., p. 147.

down a forest' cannot be ascribed to a camper whose campfire is suddenly scattered by unprecedented hurricane winds, even though but for his relatively simple act of making a fire, the forest would never have burned; and to cite the abnormal winds as causally more important factors is not to cite an excuse. Nor does one offer an excuse when he points out that Jones did not 'burn down the forest' because twelve other campfires also burned out of control and any one of them would have been sufficient to consume the whole forest. This consideration does not necessarily relieve Jones of *fault*. What it does is override the presumption that Jones's action is the crucial causal factor in the production of the outcome. But 'overriding presumptions of causal importance' and 'defeating imputations of personal fault', while of course not one and the same thing, are still sufficiently similar for their comparison to be mutually illuminating; and the discretionary character, contextual relativity, and presumptiveness of the causal ascription, while perhaps not identical with Hart's 'ascriptiveness' and 'defeasibility', are strongly analogous to them.

Simple noncausal doings, however, resist these comparisons; and to Wittgenstein's puzzling question 'What is left over if I subtract the fact that my arm goes up from the fact that I raise my arm?'[1] the notions of ascriptiveness and defeasibility can provide no answer. Here as elsewhere in philosophy, analytic techniques help to answer the penultimate questions, while the ultimate ones, being incapable of *answer*, must be come to terms with in some other way.

---

[1] Philosophical Investigations I, 621.

VII

VOLUNTARY AND INVOLUNTARY ACTS

P. J. FITZGERALD

The problem of defining an act owes its importance partly to the constant recurrence throughout the common law of a certain theme, namely the requirement of an act. This is exemplified in the Law of Contract by the proposition that acceptance must be something more than a mere mental assent; it must be by words or conduct.[1] In the Law of Torts we find that a man who has been carried bodily and against his will onto the land of another has been held not liable in trespass because there was no act on his part;[2] and in fact it has been suggested that in general a tort consists in some act done by the defendant whereby he has without just cause or excuse caused some form of harm to the plaintiff.[3] But nowhere is this requirement so clearly seen as in the Criminal Law, where it manifests itself in the rule that *mens rea* by itself is not enough to constitute a crime: there must be an *actus reus*. Even in the case of attempts to commit crimes where the criminal intent is the dominant factor, the prosecution must prove the commission of an *actus reus* sufficient to amount to an attempt.

This problem of defining an act gains further significance from the recognition by the Common Law that certain conduct, involuntary conduct, does not involve the actor in any responsibility because it is said there is in reality no act on his part. For this reason it becomes necessary to define the term 'act' to provide the test by which we can decide whether a man's conduct should involve him in any responsibility.

Difficulties arise, however, when jurists try to produce a satisfactory definition, and these difficulties are generated by the confusion of two separate questions: (1) what is an act?; and (2) when is conduct involuntary? The answer to (1) will not provide a complete solution to (2), if for no other reason than that it takes no account of the problems

From *Oxford Essays in Jurisprudence*, ed. A. G. Guest (Clarendon Press, 1961), pp. 1–28. Reprinted by permission of the author and the Clarendon Press.

[1] Anson, *Law of Contract* (21st ed.), p. 41.

[2] *Smith* v. *Stone* (1647), Stv. 65.

[3] Salmond, *Law of Torts* (12th ed.), p. 14.

of involuntary omission. Nor will the answer to (2) give us the whole answer to (1), since this question includes such problems as the place and time of an act. To answer (1), we must consider the use lawyers make of the word, and examine how far this use diverges from the ordinary usage of the word.

THE NEED FOR AN ACT

This notion of the need for an act is a complex thread and at the outset we should do well to try and disentangle some of the various strands.

(1) *Physical and mental acts.*

One such strand is the distinction between physical acts on the one hand, and thoughts, intentions, etc. on the other. This is the distinction that is being made when it is said that acceptance in the Law of Contract must be more than just a mere mental assent. Here what one might call mental acts are being excluded as not sufficient for the purpose of the law. The same is true to some extent of the need in Criminal Law for an *actus reus*, which also rules out as insufficient mere thoughts and intentions. One reason advanced for this requirement of an act is the difficulty of proof of such thoughts; as Bryan C.J. remarked, 'The intention (*l'entent*) of a man cannot be tried'. But this could hardly be a conclusive reason, for the Courts frequently decide what the accused thought and intended, and they could infer this from what he did and said. Every jury that convicts a person of larceny must be satisfied that he intended, at the time of taking, to deprive the owner permanently of the property. Another reason that is put forward is the need for objectivity. Unless there were some external, observable conduct on the part of the offeree, no-one (and especially the offeror) could tell whether the offer had been accepted or not. For, as Bryan C.J. continued, 'The devil himself knows not the intention of a man'. So until disputes and litigation arise on the matter, no-one can know (save the offeree) whether there is a contract or not.

But so far as Criminal Law is concerned, the reason why there must be an *actus reus* is partly something more important namely, the idea that to punish mere intention, and make offences of 'thought crime', is too great an intrusion into individual liberty and privacy. Although the law seeks to protect society from harmful conduct, and intentions to commit crimes are potentially harmful in that they may lead to the commission of crimes, yet the interests of the individual must be weighed and a balance must be struck between the freedom of the citizen and safety of the community. There is, however, a further difficulty that even if it were thought desirable to have such control over men's thoughts, the enforcement of such control might well be impossible.

(2) *Acts and omissions*

Another strand in this notion is the distinction between acts and omissions. Only rarely does the law impose a positive duty to act. For instance a bystander has no legal duty to save a small child from drowning. The finder of a lost article has no duty to restore it to its owner, even though he knows who the owner is. The duty not to misrepresent in the Law of Contract does not normally amount to a positive duty to disclose all the information you have. In general, the law is content to say 'Thou shalt not kill, steal or deceive'. It will not take the further step and say 'Thou shalt preserve life, restore goods to the owner, disclose all the information you have'. Before this further step is taken there must usually be shown to exist some special relationship between the parties, which gives rise to this extra positive duty. For example, the bystander must be in charge of the child. The contract must be *uberrimae fidei*. The basis of this attitude seems again to be this same reluctance of the law to encroach too much on individual liberty. While ready to penalize conduct that harms a man's neighbours, the Courts feel that to ordain the performance of conduct that will benefit one's neighbours would restrict freedom unduly and place too great a burden on the individual. So the rule that you are to love your neighbour (a positive command) is narrowed in law to the prohibition, you must not injure your neighbour.

(3) *Control*

The most difficult distinction, however, is that between acts over which a man has control, and happenings over which he has no control. There is a general principle that a man should not be punished, or have to pay damages, for occurrences over which he could exercise no control. To penalize him in this way would seem not only unfair, because he had no choice in the matter, but also inefficacious, because it would not prevent similar occurrences in the future.

Accordingly the law does not generally hold someone responsible for the operations of nature or the acts of third parties, since both these are outside his control. To hold *A* responsible for whatever harm befalls *B*, either because of the act of *C* or because of some natural event such as the falling of a tree, would be wholly unreasonable, in

the absence of special circumstances, since it would be to constitute
A an insurer of *B*'s safety. Even where *A* has himself been negligent in
the first place, he may escape liability on the ground that *C*'s act, or the
falling of the tree, amounted to a *novus actus interveniens*. On the
other hand, there are exceptions. On some occasions, despite *C*'s act
or the natural event, *A* may still be held responsible:

(i) Perhaps he should have foreseen that *C* might have done what he
did, and have taken precautions to guard against this, e.g., a man who
leaves a horse unattended in a street should foresee that mischievous
children might play with it.[1] A person who leaves the door of a house
open should foresee that thieves might enter and steal things from the
house.[2]

(ii) Or it may be that the situation created by *A* is so fraught with
danger that he must become the insurer of *B*. If *A* chooses to keep a
lion and *C* wrongfully lets it loose so that it mauls *B*, *A* will still have
to compensate *B* for his injuries.

(iii) Or the third party may in fact be someone over whom *A* has
control. *A* may for instance be already liable in negligence for failing
to keep under control his small child, if that child subsequently
injures *B*. Or the third party may be the servant of *A*, acting in the
course of his employment.

Nor is the law in general concerned with what a man is, but only with
what he does, since he may choose what he does, but not what he is.
As Holmes observed, 'It is felt to be impolitic and unjust to make a
man answerable for harm unless he might have chosen otherwise'.[4]
Here again the law is refusing to hold a man liable for something outside his control. Being found by night in a building with intention to
commit a felony therein, and kindred offences against Section 28
of the Larceny Act, 1916, are not complete exceptions to this principle, since even here there is this much choice, that the prisoner
need not have gone to or have been in that building with that intention. This is why so much dissatisfaction was aroused by the case of
Larsonneur,[5] who was convicted of being found in the United Kingdom
contrary to orders made under the Aliens Restriction Act, when in fact
she had been brought to England under police custody and was found

---

[1] *Lynch* v. *Nurdin* (1841), 1 Q.B. 29.   [2] *Stansbie* v. *Troman*, [1948] 2 K.B. 48.
[3] *Baker* v. *Snell*, [1908] 2 K.B. 352; *Behrens* v. *Bertram Mills Circus, Ltd.*, [1957]
2 Q.B. 1.   [4] Holmes. *The Common Law*, p. 45.
[5] 24 Cr. App. Rep. 74. This dissatisfaction was not felt, however, in Northern Ireland,
where the case was followed in the unreported case of *Kasriel* v. *Neumann* (1947) and
(1956), 12 N. I. L. Q., p. 61.

in a police cell, since she indeed had no choice at all in the matter.

The third and most difficult species of event over which the defendant has no control is the class of involuntary acts: the bodily movements outside his control such as reflex actions, heart beats, etc. It is chiefly this type of involuntary act that has given rise to the problem and led to the various attempts to formulate a satisfactory definition of an act in order to exclude these involuntary occurrences from liability on the ground that they are less than acts. Whereas in the first type of case where B's injury results from C's act, we say of A that it is not *his* act; in this type of case, if B's injury results from a reflex action on A's part, we say that it is not his *act*. So instead of asking what makes conduct involuntary, jurists have asked what exactly is an act.

THE DEFINITION OF AN ACT

Holmes' celebrated definition of an act as a willed muscular contraction, in which he followed Austin, contains two noteworthy features. The first of these seems at first sight, if perhaps unhelpful, at least innocuous: namely, the requirement that the muscular contraction should be willed. For a spasm, he argues, is not an act.[1] The other curious feature is the way Holmes' restricts the term 'act' to cover only the movement of the actor's muscles or limbs, and excludes from his definition everything that follows. If A shoots and kills B, according to Holmes, A's act is the willed contraction of his finger on the trigger of the gun. The firing of the gun, the bullet leaving the barrel and hitting B, and B's falling dead, these are all consequences of A's act, but not actually part of it. The reason for this oddly narrow interpretation of the term 'act', is perhaps the search for something for which to hold the actor absolutely responsible, something over which he has absolute power of control, and so complete choice. Over the firing of the gun, the bullet's hitting B, and B's falling dead, he clearly lacks this complete control, for the gun may jam; the bullet may be deflected by a sudden gust of wind; and B may be saved by the bullet lodging in the bible given to him by his great-grandmother. What Holmes calls consequences are not so entirely dependent on A, it seems, as the original act of pulling the trigger.

But if we want something completely dependent on the will of the actor, may we not be forced logically to take a further step and claim that the only thing over which A has complete control is his process of willing? He lacks this control over the firing of the gun. It is some-

[1] Holmes, op. cit., p. 54.

thing that usually ensues, but may on occasion fail, for the gun may jam. But the same could be said, surely, of A's muscular contraction when he pulls the trigger. This 'motion of the body consequent on the determination of the will', as Austin termed it, usually succeeds the act of willing (whatever that may be), but in one case in a million perhaps it might not do so, and we should recognize the onset of paralysis. Though such failure to follow may be exceedingly rare, the important fact is not the rarity, but the possibility of failure, since this suggests that the difference between A's control over the firing of the gun and his control over the contraction of his finger is only one of degree. A can be much more sure that the finger will contract than he can that the gun will fire; but he cannot be absolutely certain of either. Indeed Holmes marvelled at the 'mysterious accuracy with which the adult, who is master of himself, foresees the outward adjustment which would follow his inward effort',[1] but his view of what an act is seems to lead to the result that no adult is really master of himself at all, and that since he only *foresees* but is not certain that his muscles will obey his will, his only control is over what goes on inside his mind. But if it is only with regard to these mental acts that A is in real control, should we not then have to conclude (if we still demand that A should only be punished for actions over which he has control) that he should only be punished for his mental acts; and that it is these mental occurrences with which the law is really concerned. It is as though it were not the man we see in the dock in whom we are really interested, but rather some inner figure who pulls the strings that cause (usually) the prisoner's muscles to contract. So that we should inquire not whether A shot and killed B, nor even whether A's finger contracted and pulled the trigger due to an exercise of will on A's part, but rather whether there was a determination of the will that took place in A's mind. Yet clearly this is not the investigation that we make in the Courts. Nor does common sense dictate that it should be. Jurists have examined the notion of an act in order to illuminate the investigation we should make when faced with the problem of involuntary behaviour. The procedure should be reversed. Closer attention to the investigation we do make in cases of involuntary acts will help in effect to illuminate the notion of an act.

It might be objected that Holmes never meant to put forward a complete theory which would be thoroughly satisfactory from a philosophical point of view. All he aimed at providing us with was a rough test of what an act was; and this suffices for practical purposes.

[1] Holmes, op. cit., p. 54.

But it is for practical purposes precisely that this definition is unhelpful, because it conflicts with the general notion of what an act is. Whatever an act is, both in and out of court, we use the term in a way quite different from Holmes' way. 'Caught in the act', for example, conjures up a picture of the burglar creeping away with the swag over his shoulder; of the murderer standing over his victim, bloody knife in hand: not of a criminal contracting various muscles. So we speak of the act of stealing, and the act of shooting, and of a thousand other kinds of act. The 'act of contracting the finger' describes only the rare case when the accused tried to pull the trigger, but failed, and even here the normal description is 'the act of attempting to shoot'. This is why we demur at Holmes' conclusion that all acts are indifferent *per se* legally. Of course in his sense they must be (unless there were a statute prohibiting a certain willed muscular contraction) until we take into account the surrounding circumstances and the consequences of the contraction. But in the way we normally talk of acts it is quite untrue to say that they are legally indifferent *per se*. The reason why the act of stealing, the act of murdering, or the act of dangerous driving, are not so legally indifferent is precisely because the act in each of these cases includes all the surrounding circumstances and consequences which attract the condemnation of the law.

This restricted definition of an act is also liable to create difficulties in connexion with the question of the locality of an act. Suppose *A*, standing in state *X*, shoots at and kills *B*, standing in state *Y*, to decide whether the courts of either state have jurisdiction to try *A*, it may be necessary to decide where the murder took place. The restricted definition might lead to the conclusion that it took place in state *X*, because it was there that *A* pulled the trigger. Whereas the ordinary use of the term 'act', may allow us to say that the act was begun in state *X* and completed in state *Y*, and therefore the courts of state *Y* should have jurisdiction in such a case. And it has been held that murder is committed in the place where the death occurs.[1] This can be reconciled with Holmes' theory only by distinguishing between the crime of murder and the act (pulling the trigger) which is only part of the crime. Yet the courts do not seem to distinguish in this way, as may be seen perhaps from the case of *R.* v. *Jarmain*.[2] Here the argument was that since the accused's gun fired without his consciously pulling the trigger, there was no act on his part and therefore he was not guilty of murder. The Court of Criminal Appeal, however, held that there

[1] *R.* v. *Coombes* (1786), 1 Leach 388; Salmond, *Jurisprudence* (11th ed.), p. 406.
[2] [1946] K.B. 74.

was an act on his part, namely the act of robbery with violence and that as death resulted the accused was guilty.

Hence Salmond asserted that 'an act has no *natural* boundaries, any more than an event or a place has. Its limits must be artificially defined for the purpose in hand for the time being. It is for the law to determine, in each particular case, what circumstances and what consequences shall be counted within the compass of the act with which it is concerned. To ask what act a man has done is like asking in what place he lives.'[1] He also argued that the distinction between an act and its consequences is merely a verbal one; a matter of convenience of speech. But the fact that the question may be verbal does not entail that it is trivial. If the word 'act' were used in such a way that without a willed muscular contraction there is no act, Jarmain might not have been hanged. Indeed, it is true to say that many of the problems facing the courts are verbal problems. Once the facts have been found, e.g. that A stabbed B and Dr. C failed to treat B adequately, and B died, then the Court has to decide whether on these facts it would be right to say that A caused B's death. Similarly, if A, intending to burn B's haystack, takes out of his pocket a box of matches and runs over to the stack and then does no more, the court must decide whether, if these facts are proved, they amount to attempted arson. In all these cases, after the factual dispute has been settled, there then arises what may be called the verbal dispute, the problem of classifying the defendant's conduct—is what he did to count as murder, attempted arson, etc.? But none of these disputes are any the less difficult, or important, for being verbal.

The difficulty of such verbal disputes stems from the fact that the general meaning of the terms, e.g. 'attempt', 'murder', 'cause', has been set and, though it may be hard to draw the line in a given case, it is easy to find cases well to one side or other of the line. What the courts have to decide is whether the features of the border-line case are more akin to the cases on the one side or to those on the other. And remembering the important consequences that will follow from their decision, they must be guided by various principles in deciding with which group of cases to classify the border-line case. What the court is not free to do is to define the word (attempt, murder, cause) as it pleases. With regard to the problem of defining an act, it has been said that a person is free to define a word as he pleases.[2] One is free to do so, provided one remembers (and one never does) that this arbitrary

---

[1] Salmond, *Jurisprudence* (11th ed.), pp. 401-2.

[2] Dias & Hughes, *Jurisprudence*, p. 202.

way of using the word is different from the usual way of using it, and that when lawyers ask what is an act, they are concerned with the way the term is used in legal argument, and not with any special use that some writer might decide to make of the term.

One reason for the unhelpfulness of trying to elucidate criteria of responsibility by demanding an act on the defendant's part, and then by defining what an act is, is that it reverses to some extent the procedure of ordinary language, because in ordinary speech the word 'act', together with such allied expressions as 'A did it', is used not so much to describe what has happened, as to ascribe responsibility.[1] In so far as the word 'act' is not being used to mark such distinctions as those referred to above, e.g. the distinction between acts and omissions; between acts and words (actions speak louder than words); or between acts, words and thoughts (we sin in thought, word and deed) the word is used to impute responsibility. 'A's act caused B's death' is less a way of describing what has happened, than another way of saying that it was A's fault. 'It was not A's act at all' (e.g. because he was having an epileptic fit) is another way of saying that we should not blame A in this case because of some special feature in the situation.

Holmes suggested that the special feature was the lack of volition. One drawback of this approach is that it suggests that what we investigate in each case is whether the bodily movement was preceded or accompanied by some interior process. In certain cases it may be that before a man does something he goes through some such process of setting himself to do it, e.g. if it is something very difficult to do, but the vast majority of cases where a man does something do not contain any such feature, nor do we look for one when we consider his conduct, whether in court or out of court.

A further difficulty arises with regard to omissions. In those cases where a man is held criminally or civilly liable for an omission, it is quite clear that he may be held liable even though he never applied his mind to the matter at all. In fact he may be held liable just for not having applied his mind. There may be, of course, the rare case where he might deliberately refuse to apply his mind, or where he might deliberately refrain from doing what the law enjoins; but the usual case of omission is that of the man who just fails to act without thinking about it at all. And here it is quite untrue to say that there has been any process of willing. Any test of responsibility must surely take into

[1] H. L. A. Hart, *The Ascription of Responsibility and Rights* (1948–9), Proc. Arist. Soc. 179.

account the case of omissions, and just as there are cases where a man may not be held responsible for what he had done, e.g. while asleep, so there are cases where he may not be held responsible for what he has omitted to do; and the principle seems to be the same in both types of case. The real problem here is to see what is the minimum requirement of the law before a man can be held responsible, either for his act or for his omission.

VOLUNTARY AND INVOLUNTARY ACTS

The common method of stating this minimum requirement is to assert that there must be a voluntary act on the defendant's part.[1] This attempt to solve the problem, however, is no more helpful with regard to omissions, than is the definition of an act put forward by Holmes. It is a curious description of a thoughtless omission, to say that it is something voluntary on the part of the defendant. In any such cases of omission, there has been nothing on his part at all: so that it is difficult to see how one can sensibly talk here of a voluntary nothing.[2] The demand that the act should be voluntary confuses two different distinctions.

There is, it is true, a very important distinction between what a man does voluntarily and what he does under compulsion, duress, necessity, etc. Before admitting a confession in evidence, for example, the Judge may have to determine whether it was voluntary, or whether it was obtained by some threat or inducement. Or again, we may excuse someone of a crime on the ground that the accused was not acting voluntarily, but under duress. A woman's husband may have coerced her into acting as she did. In these cases the accused did have a choice; there was no need to make the confession, or to do what was done. But the choice was so difficult that we feel that the confession should be not admitted. For the inducement of bail, for example, may have led the accused to make a false confession. Or the husband's coercion may have made it difficult for the wife to choose to act otherwise than as she did.

[1] Cross & Jones, *Criminal Law* (3rd ed.), p. 32; Kenny, *Outlines of Criminal Law* (17th ed.), pp. 26–7; American Law Institute's *Model Penal Code, Tentative Draft No. 4*, Art. 2, s. 2.0 (1); *cf*; Queensland Code, s. 23; Tasmanian Code, s. 13 (1); Stephen, *History of the Criminal Law of England*, Vol. *II*, p. 97; Barry, Paton & Sawer, *Criminal Law in Australia* (1948), p. 48.

[2] Cf., Perkins (1939), 52 Harv. L.R. 912; Glanville Williams, *Criminal Law*, p. 15. Nevertheless it is not true to say that the idea of a voluntary omission makes no sense—one can be compelled to omit to do something, and equally one can omit to do it voluntarily.

But there is a totally different distinction: the distinction between normal conduct and involuntary movements of the body, such as the beating of one's heart, spasms, what one does in sleep, etc. In these cases there is no question of choice at all. Now the voluntary act theory blurs this important difference[1] and obscures the real question, namely, why it is that the courts refuse to hold a person liable in certain cases on the ground that his act or omission was involuntary. What is the test by which we distinguish these acts and omissions from the normal acts and omissions?

The search for the answer to these questions may best be conducted by first considering the types of behaviour that have been recognized as involuntary by the courts in different branches of the law. Then we may inquire whether there is any common criterion for determining whether in general behaviour is involuntary. Thirdly, there will arise the question why different branches of the law do, and should, treat these types of involuntary behaviour differently from normal behaviour.

TYPES OF INVOLUNTARY ACTION RECOGNIZED BY LAW

These fall into two main categories.

(a) Where the defendant is compelled to do what he does by some external force; and

(b) Where he is compelled by some internal force, or where at least the compulsion is not due to any external cause.

Where the defendant is physically compelled by some external force, either by some other person or by some force of nature to act as he does, courts have recognized this type of case as exonerating the defendant from liability. So in the Criminal Law 'If A takes B's arm and the weapon in his hand and stabs C, B would be not guilty because there was no voluntary act on his part.'[2] Such a defence would also be raised in the case of an omission, where, for example, A, a parent, under a legal duty to rescue B, his child, from drowning, is forcibly prevented by C from so doing. In tort the same rule has been applied:

[1] 'Voluntary' and 'Involuntary' are not opposites, as was pointed out by J. L. Austin in 'A Plea for Excuses' (1956–7), Proc. Arist. Soc. Cf., Bentham, Principles of Morals and Legislation, p. 82; see also Jerome Hall, Principles of Criminal Law, p. 522. Stephen opposed 'voluntary' to 'involuntary', however, and not to 'compelled', op. cit., pp. 101–2.

[2] 1 Hale, P.C. 434, 472; Blackstone, Commentaries on the Laws of England, Vol. IV. p. 27; cp., 1 Hawk, P.C., ch. 29, s. 3.

where for instance a defendant was carried by a gang of armed men on to the plaintiff's premises, he was held not liable in trespass.[1] It is important to distinguish this case of physical compulsion, as it is sometimes called, from the case of duress. If the defence is duress, then the defendant is pleading that, though he had a choice, the alternative to doing what he did was so hard that it is too much to ask of any man that he should choose the alternative. The accused has no say in how his arm moves: it is moved for him. This is the difference between the case suggested by Hale and the case of *R.* v. *Bourne,*[2] the decision in which is only explicable on the basis that the wife herself had committed a crime. Similarly, in *Gilbert* v. *Stone*[3] a defendant compelled by threat of injury to enter the plaintiff's premises was held liable in trespass.

That people's acts may be involuntary without the compulsion of any external force is a fact that has become increasingly clearer with the growth of medical science. As Paton observed,[4] 'medicine, psychoanalysis and psychiatry are opening new doors and the law will gradually be forced to reconsider the theories on which its analysis of an act is based'. The best known of these internally motivated involuntary acts are those of epileptics undergoing fits of convulsions, and it is no accident that the word 'epileptic' was coined by the Greeks to signify something that might fall on a man, something that seized him from within himself.[5] These involuntary acts may be roughly divided into (a) movements over which nobody has control; and (b) movements over which people normally do have control, but over which a particular defendant lacks control because of some abnormality.[6]

---

[1] *Smith* v. *Stone* (1647), Sty. 65.

[2] (1952), 36 Cr. App. Rep. 125. See Cross in (1953), 69 L.Q.R., p. 354, but Lord Goddard stresses at p. 128 that '(the plea of duress) means that she admits that she has committed the crime', and at p. 129 that 'the offence of buggery ... does not depend on consent: it depends on the act, and if an act of buggery is committed, the felony is committed'.

[3] (1647), Sty. 72; Aleyn 35.

[4] Paton, *Jurisprudence* (2nd ed.), p. 243.

[5] For a useful medical account of such conditions see Penfield and Jasper, *Epilepsy and the Functional Anatomy of the Human Brain* (1954). See also Gowers, *Diseases of the Nervous System, II* (1893), pp. 746–9; Henderson and Gillespie, *A Textbook of Psychiatry* (8th ed.).

[6] The first sub-class may be sub-divided into:
(i) the movement of his body of which a man knows nothing without observation, e.g. heart beats, the peristaltic movement of the gut;

There is little authority in law on the first class of involuntary acts, partly because it is unlikely that such uncontrollable movements should result in any harm, and even if they did, it is so clear that a person would not be held liable for such harm that prosecution would hardly be launched. Since the tort of trespass to the person now would seem to require intention or negligence on the part of the defendant,[1] it is unlikely that a defendant in such circumstances would be sued in tort either. Writers such as Austin, Bentham and Stephen, agree in classifying all these movements as involuntary and not deserving of punishment.[2] The American Law Institute's Model Penal Code defines certain types of acts as not voluntary, among which are reflexes or convulsions, and the Code contains a final omnibus class excluding as not voluntary any bodily movements that otherwise are not products of the effort or determination of the actor, either conscious or habitual.[3]

With regard to the type of movements over which people do normally have control, but over which a particular defendant lacked control because of some abnormality, the abnormality may be his unconsciousness, e.g. he may be merely asleep, and in sleep, it is said, there is no sin. 'Acts done by a person asleep cannot be criminal, there being no consciousness.'[4] Similarly, it is unlikely for instance, in the law of tort that a man would be held liable for slander, for defamatory words spoken in his sleep.[5] Likewise, the acts of a man under somnambulism will not render him guilty of any crime.[6] But the abnormality may be that the defendant's behaviour is due to disease or injury. In *R.* v. *Charlson*[7] a father who in a fit of automatism seriously injured his small son was found not guilty of any crime since the jury was not satisfied that he might not have

(ii) movements which he does know about without observation, e.g. twitches, ticks, jerks etc. (where the cause itself, however, is known only by observation and reflex actions, such as the jerking of one's knee when it is tapped by a doctor, or a sudden leaping back when attacked by a wild animal).
See G. E. Anscombe, *Intention*, pp. 13ff.

[1] *Fowler* v. *Lanning*, [1959] 1 Q.B. 426.

[2] Austin, *Jurisprudence*, I. 360, 415, 419, 498; Bentham, op. cit., p. 164, 171, 174–5; Stephen, op. cit., p. 99.

[3] Model Penal Code, Art. 2, s. 2.0 (2) (d).

[4] MacDonald, *The Criminal Law of Scotland* (5th ed.), p. 11.

[5] Pollock on Torts (15th ed.), p. 47.

[6] Wharton, *Criminal Law* (12th ed.), *I*, s. 84; Russell on Crime (11th ed.), p. 40; Glanville Williams, op. cit., p. 14. See *R.* v. *Minor* (1955), 112 Can. C.C. 29.

[7] [1955] 1 All E.R. 859.

been acting as he did on account of a brain tumour; and so they were not satisfied that he had any choice as to his actions. Similarly, a man who killed his mother when his consciousness was clouded as a result of hypoglycaemia, was found not guilty of murder.[1] In these cases the lack of control arises because of lack of consciousness, as in cases of sleep-walking where the defendant does not know what he is doing. It may be, however, that he knows what he is doing and is yet quite incapable of exercising any control. Sufferers from fits of ictal or post-ictal conditions arising from epilepsy or injury have been known to describe their experiences by saying that though they knew in a sort of way what they were doing, yet they felt that all their actions were being controlled by some external force, as though by some remote control station.[2]

A very difficult problem is posed where the abnormal lack of control is due not to disease or injury, but to drunkenness or drugs. Involuntary drunkenness, *i.e.* where *A* secretly and against *B*'s will administers intoxicating liquor to *B*, is always said to be a defence.[3] Where, however, the accused himself was responsible for getting drunk, he will only be excused either if he is so drunk as to be insane within the McNaghten rules, or if he is incapable of forming a specific intent required by the courts. It is no defence that his intoxication made him more easily lose control of himself.[4] As to acts done under hypnotism or post-hypnotic suggestion, there is little authority.[5] The American Law Institute classifies 'conduct during hypnosis, or resulting from hypnotic suggestion' as involuntary. But the difficulty is that it is not clear how far a hypnotized person can be tricked into doing something dishonest or felonious.[6] On the other hand, such a subject might well be tricked into doing some dangerous act by being persuaded that he was in fact doing an act of quite a different kind, e.g. the hypnotist might tell him to shoot someone with a water pistol while placing in his hand a real loaded pistol. But here the defence would not be so much that the defendant had no ability

[1] *Lancet* (1943), Vol. 1 pp. 526–7.

[2] Cf., defendant's account in *Buckley & T.T.C.* v. *Smith Transport*, [1946] 4 D.L.R. 721.

[3] *R.* v. *Pearson* (1835), 2 Lew, C.C. 144; 1 Hale 32.

[4] *D.P.P.* v. *Beard*, [1920] A.C. 479; *R.* v. *McCarthy*, [1954] 2 Q.B. 105.

[5] Glanville Williams, op. cit., p. 12.

[6] See Taylor, *Principles and Practice of Medical Jurisprudence* (11th ed.), Experiments were carried out on 50 subjects, all of whom awoke rather than perform some repugnant act: J. R. Rees, *Modern Practice in Psychiatric Medicine* (1949), p. 391.

to control his movements, as that he did not fully appreciate the nature of his act.

What emerges from a survey of these different types of case is that the common minimal requirement of the law seems to be that the accused should have had the ability to control his movements.

CRIMINAL LAW

The most important field of law where problems arise with regard to involuntary acts is the Criminal Law. The attraction of stating the defence of involuntariness in terms of there being no act on the part of the accused is that this will be a defence even in cases of strict liability. To group this minimal requirement of power of control with the *actus reus* instead of with *mens rea*, means that a person who fails to conform to a halt sign because of a fit of automatism is not guilty of an offence, whereas one who fails because his brakes failed, or because he could not see the sign, would be guilty.[1]

The reason for the Criminal Law's insistence on this minimal requirement of ability of control is that the way in which the Criminal Law seeks to protect society from harmful conduct is in general by imposing penalties to deter would-be criminals. The imposition of penalties for involuntary acts cannot, of course, serve to prevent people from committing such involuntary acts. Furthermore, in the case of involuntary acts there arises no question of what Bentham termed the secondary mischief, i.e. the general effect on the community of the wrongful act, since in general if the accused acted involuntarily, there is no reason for the public to be apprehensive as to his future conduct in the same way as if he had behaved freely and willingly. Consequently, to use Bentham's phraseology, punishment would be both inefficacious and groundless. Inefficacious in that it could not prevent the primary mischief (since we cannot help our involuntary acts), and groundless because there is no secondary mischief to prevent.[2]

[1] *Hill* v. *Baxter*, [1958] 1 Q. B. 277; Edwards (1958), 21 M.L.R. 375; there are also repercussions from this grouping in the law of evidence, as was shown by *R.* v. *Harrison Owen*, [1951] 2 All E.R. 726; see Cowen & Carter, *Essays on the Law of Evidence*, pp. 111–4; Cross, *Evidence*, 287–8; Glanville Williams, op. cit., p. 14. The latter suggests that there are few offences of strict liability where the defence of involuntariness could apply, but road traffic offences are an exception to this contention.

[2] Bentham, op. cit., pp. 164, 171, 174–5, 315. It could be argued that punishment would be equally inefficacious in the case of the motorist whose brakes failed or who failed to observe the halt sign, but surely here the justification could be that punishment might cause him to test his brakes regularly and keep a keener look-out in future.

But not only is it therefore impolitic to punish such conduct, it is also unjust. Without inquiring too deeply into the moral justification for punishment, we may recognize the existence of a moral principle that we should not blame or punish one who could not help doing what he did. That this is a separate matter from that of deterrence can be seen from the following consideration. One can imagine that the punishment of involuntary conduct might possibly serve to deter would-be criminals in this way: While not preventing future involuntary conduct, it might prevent conduct that is not involuntary, if potential criminals said to themselves: 'See, this Draconian code even punishes those who cannot help stealing—the kleptomaniacs too. We, therefore, who can help stealing would be shown no mercy, so we had better refrain from committing crimes altogether.' Yet nobody would deny that, even if crimes could be prevented in this way, it would be unjust to punish those who cannot help what they do; and this it seems is the flaw in any theory of punishment based wholly on deterrence.

On the other hand there are cases where although the accused lacks the ability to control what he does, secondary mischief will arise and the community will be apprehensive about his future behaviour. Such cases are those where the accused's condition resulted from earlier conduct of his, over which he did have control. Stephen made this point clearly when he urged that the law ought to be that no act is a crime if the person who does it is at the time when it is done prevented, either by defective mental power or by disease affecting his mind, from controlling his own conduct, unless the absence of power of control is brought about by his own fault.[1] For this reason the courts have always leaned against allowing drunkenness as a defence when the accused allowed himself to get into a state of intoxication. Here it is felt that if he did this once he might well do it again, and men must be deterred from allowing themselves to get into such a condition. It is precisely because there was an earlier stage when the accused could have helped what he did, that punishment will serve some purpose. Likewise, if fumes suddenly overcome the driver of a motor car and the car swerves across the road into another vehicle, the driver will not be guilty of dangerous driving. But if he falls asleep at the wheel without any such external cause, then we could say that there was an earlier stage when he was driving dangerously, in that he continued to drive although he felt himself becoming drowsy. At this

[1] Stephen, op. cit., p. 168. Cp., Wharton, *Criminal Law* (12th ed.), I, s. 84; *Lewis* v. *State* (1943), 196 Ga. 755.

point he could have taken action either to ensure that he kept awake, or he could have stopped driving and waited until his somnolence had passed. This technique of moving back to a stage at which the defendant had a choice will sometimes enable lawyers to differentiate between cases where no blame should attach to the defendant because he could not help doing what he did, and cases where he is culpable because he could have avoided getting into the state where he was unable to help acting as he did. So we can say in a case such as *Hill* v. *Baxter*[1] that if the defendant was to blame for not forcing himself to stay awake, or for not stopping until he felt fit to drive, it was at this earlier stage that he was committing the crime of dangerous driving, rather than at the later stage when he actually was asleep. But this technique runs into difficulties with regard to omissions. For if the defendant argues that he is not guilty of failing to conform to a traffic sign because he was unconscious, we can hardly differentiate between the case where fumes suddenly bereft him of consciousness, and the case where he just fell asleep, by saying that in the latter case there was an earlier point of time where he was failing to conform. It is not yet clear how the courts will distinguish between these two types of case, but perhaps it can be suggested that where fumes overcome the driver he should be acquitted, not on the ground that there was no act on his part, but on the ground that he was unable to prevent himself from falling asleep, and at the same time there was no warning of what was going to happen, so that both his dangerous driving and his failure to conform to the traffic sign were involuntary. Where, however, he realizes he is falling asleep, has some warning, and yet takes no precautions, then this defence should not be open to him. The term 'involuntary' can then be reserved for those cases where no ability to control his actions arises at any stage;[2] and this defence of involuntariness should be excluded in cases where the accused either brought about his own lack of power of control, or foresaw that he might lack control and took no precautions. Here culpability and deterrence go hand-in-hand, for we feel that where there was the power of choice at an earlier stage, and the defendant could have helped it, he is culpable; and we also feel that punishment will serve to deter people from similar behaviour in the future. This, to some extent, supports the

[1] [1958] 1 Q. B. 277.

[2] i.e., once he has commenced a course of conduct, for otherwise the suggested test would exclude even the case of the motorist overcome by fumes, since he could have always abstained from driving, and so the test would become vacuous.

decision in *Jarmain's case*.[1] Even if he had no choice as to whether the gun went off or not, nevertheless he did have some say in the question whether or not to commit armed robbery, so that he was to some extent responsible, and his punishment would deter others from committing this crime.

There are, however, cases where there is no choice at all on the defendant's part, but his condition is such that he is liable to cause harm to others. Epileptics, for example, cannot help the fits they have. But if they know that they are likely to injure others in the course of these fits, it may not be wholly unreasonable to demand that they refrain from engaging in activities where the onset of a fit might lead to disastrous injury to other people. Such harm could clearly ensue if a fit overtook an epileptic in the course of driving a car, and for this reason the Motor Vehicle (Driving Licence) Regulations, 1950, prohibit epileptics from obtaining a driving licence.[2] Similarly a diabetic who fails to take sufficient food and suffers from an insulin reaction may not unreasonably be convicted of driving under the influence of drugs, even though this was not perhaps the type of case originally envisaged by the Road Traffic Acts.[3] In these cases the defendant could not help the onset of the fits, or the insulin reaction. Nor is it true to say that his lack of control of his action is in any way due to anything he had done. But since he knows of the possible dangers, he should refrain from certain types of activity: and here choice does come into play, for he can choose, for instance, whether or not to drive a motor-car in the first place. He is not, therefore, absolutely justified in saying, 'I could not help what happened'. Here too, therefore, there is a stage at which we can say that he had some choice as to what has occurred.

There may, however, even be cases where there is no choice at all on the part of the accused. So far we have discussed two cases where a man cannot help acting as he does:

(*a*) where his inability arose from previous behaviour which he could have helped; and

(*b*) where his inability is no fault of his but, knowing that he is unable to help behaving as he does, he should avoid putting himself in a position where his involuntary behaviour may injure others; and he could so avoid putting himself into this position.

[1] *Supra*, p. 9.
[2] Regulation 5.
[3] See *The New Scientist*, 4th June, 1959, p. 1244.

There is, however, the third case: that of the man who cannot help his involuntary behaviour, and cannot avoid putting himself in the position where his involuntary behaviour may injure others; and whose involuntary actions may be so dangerous to the community that deterrence gives place to prevention. The fits of an epileptic may be so dangerous that we no longer merely feel that he ought to refrain from certain activities requiring special care and skill, such as driving. It may even be necessary to confine him in order to prevent him altogether from mixing with other people. At this stage we begin to leave the question of punishment and turn to the question of what we should do to protect society from possible danger. Deterrents and correction no longer have any effect, and prevention is the only remedy.[1]

CIVIL LIABILITY

The way that the courts deal with involuntary acts with regard to civil liability is not necessarily the same as the way of the Criminal Law. How far lack of ability to control one's movements exempts a defendant from liability in tort is bound up with the question whether liability in tort is based on fault or not. In so far as liability depends on fault, clearly involuntary acts or omissions on the part of the defendant should not render him liable, for a person is not at fault for doing what he cannot help doing. Accordingly, nobody should be held liable in negligence for an act or omission which he could not help, unless his inability to avoid the act or omission is due to some previous act or omission over which he does have control. A lunatic, therefore, could plead as a defence to negligence that he was not guilty of a breach of duty of care owing to the plaintiff, since the act or omission complained of was involuntary, and therefore

---

[1] Prevention can often be seen as the basis of punishment, e.g., in preventive detention, imposed when a court concludes from the prisoner's record that he is beyond reform and the only course is to lock him up so that he can no longer get at other people's property; in the incarceration of the guilty but insane; in the death penalty, and in the older penalties of transportation and mutilation; and in the more modern penalty of disqualification from driving. On the ground that the community must be protected, it may not be unreasonable that a man suffering so frequently from epileptic fits as to be dangerous should, if he raises a defence of automatism, run the risk of the prosecution contending that his condition brings him within the McNaghten Rules, as in *R.* v. *Kemp,* [1957] 1 Q.B. 399. Cf., Henderson & Gillespie, op. cit., p. 683, where it is contended that it is not justifiable to certify a man in the course of an epileptic fit. Contrast the South African decision *R.* v. *Mkize,* 1959 (2) S.A. 260 (N).

could not constitute such a breach.[1] (It is submitted that this is a more satisfactory approach to the problem than to contend that the lunatic does not owe the same duty of care as the reasonable man). An intoxicated man could not put forward such an argument because, if his breach of duty of care was involuntary, it resulted from his previous negligence in allowing himself to get into a state of intoxication.[2]

How far, however, is the fact that the defendant's behaviour was involuntary, a defence to torts of strict liability? Since the courts appear inclined to restrict trespass to the person to intentional or negligent acts,[3] and since inevitable accident is accepted as a defence to trespass to goods,[4] clearly an involuntary trespass would be a defence to either of these actions: though the courts may well have to distinguish between the case where this was due to no fault of the defendant, and the case where the defendant brought about his own inability to control his movements. With regard to trespass to land, it has been held that involuntary trespass, where the defendant could not help what he was doing, is a defence.[5] Even in those cases of strict liability, therefore, the lack of ability to control one's movements seems to operate as a defence. For liability may be so strict as not to allow a defendant to plead that he was mistaken, e.g. that he did not know that the land was not his own, but it does not force the courts to award damages against a man who had no choice at all as to what he did. This gives point to the above quoted defence of tort, that it is in general an act, for as Holmes remarked, an act implies choice.[6]

Even where the law of tort appears to be based purely on the need to compensate the plaintiff for the injury he has suffered, as in the ruling on. *Rylands* v. *Fletcher* (though even here, the defence of act of God, or act of a third party, will avail), or in the Scienter

[1] Clerk & Lindsell on Torts (11th ed.), pp. 92–3: Salmond, *Law of Torts* (12th ed.), 76: Street, *Law of Torts*, p. 500: Pollock, *Law of Torts* (15th ed.), p. 47; Winfield, *Law of Tort* (6th ed.), p. 130; *Morriss* v. *Marsden*, [1952] 1 All E.R. 925: Todd (1952), 15 M.L.R. 486. Cf., *White* v. *White*, [1950] P. 39, at p. 52.

[2] Even in Negligence, however, liability is not wholly dependent on fault, as can be seen from the objective standard, whereby an abnormally stupid or abnormally clumsy man cannot be heard to say that, being unable to help being stupid or clumsy, he should not be held liable. See Holmes, op. cit. 107 ff., Prosser, *Torts* (2nd ed.), 118, 29, and American Restatement of the Law of Torts, I. 2.

[3] *Fowler* v. *Lanning, supra*, p. 15.

[4] *N.C.B.* v. *Evans*; [1951] 2 K.B. 861.

[5] *Smith* v. *Stone (supra)*, cf., *Beckwith* v. *Shordike* (1767), 4 Burr. 2092.

[6] Holmes, op. cit., p. 54: cf., Pollock, *op. cit.*, p. 47.

action (where the wrongful act of a third party will not avail the defendant as a defence), nevertheless it seems that there must be some power of control exercisable at some stage by the defendant. The principle is, in these cases, that the defendant has created the dangerous situation and should therefore compensate a plaintiff who suffers harm as a result. The defendant need not have brought in and accumulated the water on his land. He need not have kept a ferocious animal. But where the bringing in of the water, or the keeping of the animal was not done by the defendant, it would be contrary to common sense to hold him responsible. Otherwise, 'Why need the defendant have acted at all, and why is it not enough that his existence has been at the expense of the plaintiff?'[1]

Involuntary conduct also raises problems with regard to causation. A conscious act on the part of the plaintiff will in general snap the chain of causation, whereas if the act is involuntary, the resulting harm may still be laid at the door of the defendant. So if A injures B who, as a result of the injury, commits suicide, A may be liable to B's dependants under the Fatal Accidents Act, provided the deceased's condition was such that his act is regarded as involuntary.[2] Similarly, if A puts B in such a position of peril that he acts involuntarily, and so makes matters worse, A will be both civilly and criminally liable for the harm resulting to B.[3] This same principle is found at work in the rescue cases.

EVIDENCE

In the law of evidence, however, different questions arise with regard to involuntary acts which, in this context, comprise involuntary statements. The question is no longer whether the defendant should be held responsible for his involuntary behaviour, but whether any admission made involuntarily should be allowed in evidence against a party. The generally accepted reason for excluding statements made out of court as evidence to prove the truth of what they assert, is twofold:[4] (a) because such statements were not made on oath, and therefore may not be trustworthy; and (b) because there is no possibility of their veracity or correctness

[1] Ibid., p. 95.

[2] Pigney v. Pointer's Transport Services, [1957] 2 All E.R. 807.

[3] R. v. Pitts (1842), Car. & M. 284; Hart & Honoré (1956), 72 L.Q.R. 272; Salmond, Law of Torts, p. 735, and cases there noted.

[4] Cross, Evidence, p. 350; Wigmore on Evidence, s. 1048.

being decided by cross-examination. Admissions are, however, allowed as evidence against a party because (i) though not on oath, they are likely to be true since they were against the interest of the man who made them; and (ii) because the party who made them will have an opportunity by his own evidence to explain the circumstances, and show how much reliance is to be placed on them; and this will serve the purpose normally served by cross-examination. Admissions made in sleep, therefore, or in delirium, or under hypnosis, could it seems be admissible on this reasoning. Suppose, for example, the prisoner is charged with burgling premises, and denies ever having visited these premises; if he talks in his sleep and describes these premises, should this admission necessarily be excluded? The prisoner will be able to explain the statement and these circumstances (so that the objection of lack of cross-examination is met), and there is no reason to suppose that the statement (if against interest) is untrue. Such admissions have been received.[1] On the other hand, when the prisoner is arrested he must be cautioned that he need not say anything; consequently if he is in a state of delirium and cannot help saying what he does, perhaps it is only fair that anything he says in custody in such conditions should not be received in evidence against him. Otherwise he would be denied the choice offered to him by the law, the right not to say anything.[2]

Confessions, on the other hand, raise a different problem. Here the law of evidence lays down that a confession must be voluntary, i.e. it must not be obtained by force, threats, or inducement, since in such cases there is always the danger that such confessions may be false. That this is the principle seems to emerge from the fact that where the confession is obtained by fraud (as opposed to threats or inducement) it is not thereby excluded, because it is not thereby any the more likely to be untrue.[3] A confession that is involuntary, however, in that it is obtained by means of hypnosis or truth drugs cannot be excluded on this ground, for so far from the prisoners being induced to speak falsely, it may be that he is being forced to speak

[1]Wigmore, op. cit., s. 500 Cp., Gardiner & Lansdown, *South African Criminal Law and Procedure* (6th ed.), I, pp. 597, 603, 605; in S. Africa confessions to be admissible, must be made by the accused in sound and sober senses. But cf. *R.* v. *Lincoln*, 1950 P.H., H. 68 (A.D.) Contrast Indian Evidence Act, 1872, s. 29—a confession is not irrelevant because the accused is drunk or has been deceived.

[2]Wigmore, op. cit., s. 841 ; Indian Evidence Act. 1872, s. 29.

[3]See Inbau, *Journal of Criminal Law and Criminology* (1934), XXIV. 1153: Mosier & Hames, ibid, (1935), XXVI, 431.

the truth. At present, however, medical experts are not agreed as to the success of hypnosis or the truth drug,[1] The former, it is suggested, involves the danger that the accused may agree to anything that is suggested to him. A confession made while drunk has been received in evidence,[2] but in an American case where the Sheriff deliberately made a prisoner drunk in order to obtain the confession, it was excluded.[3] This suggests the existence of another principle, that confessions obtained by removing from the defendant any choice as to what he says, should be excluded, not because they are any the less likely to be true, but because of the interference with personal liberty. To allow in evidence confessions obtained in such a manner would not only be serving to facilitate just the sort of police activity which the courts are astute to prevent, but would be inconsistent with the general principle of our legal system, which gives the prisoner the choice of whether to give evidence in court or not. It would be inconsistent with this principle to force the prisoner to make a confession and give evidence against himself outside the court, when you cannot force him to give evidence in the witness box. Indeed, in England, the Judges' rules require that a prisoner should first be cautioned that he need not say anything.[4] To get a confession from him against his will (even though the confession were clearly true) would contravene this principle of giving the prisoner the option of silence.

CONCLUSION

In conclusion, it may be said:

(1) that the correct definition of the word 'act' is to be found by looking at the use made of the word by lawyers. It is used partly to mark certain distinctions and partly to ascribe responsibility.

(2) that this question should be kept separate from the other question, namely, in what circumstances does an act or omission fail to attract liability (criminal or civil) on the ground that it is involuntary. The answer to this may be found by examining the types of behaviour

[1] In R. v. Booher, [1928] 4 D.L.R. 795 a confession following an alleged hypnotic suggestion was excluded.

[2] Vaughan's Trial (1696), 13 How. St. Tr. 507 : R. v. Spisbury (1835), 7 C. & P. 187.

[3] McNutt v. State (1903), 68 Nebr. 207.

[4] Archbold, Criminal Pleading, Evidence and Practice (33rd ed.), p. 414, Rules 4 & 5. See Silving (1956), 69 Harv. L.R. 693.

recognized as involuntary, by searching for a connecting quality, and by considering how far different branches of the law treat such involuntary behaviour differently from normal behaviour. The common quality connecting all these types of behaviour would seem to be inability to control one's bodily movements, i.e. in the case of an act, inability to avoid doing it; in the case of an omission, inability to do the act prescribed by law, provided that this inability is not the result of previous behaviour which was under the actor's control. How far the law treats, or ought to treat, such behaviour differently depends upon the purpose and principles of different branches of the law. It must be remembered that the considerations to be borne in mind in criminal cases are not necessarily the same as in actions in tort or in divorce, or yet again in the cases referred to above raised by the law of evidence.

VIII

INTENTION

G. E. M. ANSCOMBE

WHAT distinguishes actions which are intentional from those which are not? The answer that suggests itself is that they are the actions to which a certain sense of the question 'Why'? is given application; the sense is defined as that in which the answer, *if positive*, gives a reason for acting. But this hardly gets us any further, because the questions 'What is the relevant sense of the question "Why"?' and 'What is meant by "reason for acting"?' are one and the same.

To see the difficulties here, consider the question 'Why did you knock the cup off the table'? answered by 'I thought I saw a face at the window and it made me jump'. Now we cannot say that since the answer mentions something previous to the action, this will be a cause as opposed to a reason; for if you ask 'Why did you kill him'? the answer 'he killed my father' is surely a reason rather than a cause, but what it mentions is previous to the action. It is true that we don't ordinarily think of a case like giving a sudden start when we speak of a *reason for acting*. 'Giving a sudden start', someone might say, 'is not *acting* in the sense suggested by the expression "reason for acting".' Hence, though indeed we readily say e.g. 'What was the reason for your starting so violently'? this is totally unlike 'What is your reason for excluding so-and-so from your will'? or 'What is your reason for sending for a taxi'? But what *is* the difference? Why is giving a start or gasp not an 'action', while sending for a taxi or crossing the road is one? The answer cannot be 'Because an answer to the question "why"? may give a reason in the latter cases', for the answer may 'give a reason' in the former cases too; and we cannot say 'Ah, but not a *reason for acting*'; we should be going round in circles. We need to find the difference between the two kinds of 'reason' without talking about 'acting'; and if we do, perhaps we shall discover what is meant by 'acting' when it is said with this special emphasis.

It will hardly be enlightening to say 'in the case of the sudden

From *Proceedings of the Aristotelian Society*, Vol. 57 (1956–7), pp. 321–32. Reprinted by courtesy of the author and the Editor of the Aristotelian Society.

start the "reason" is a *cause*'; the topic of causality is in a state of too great confusion; all we know is that this is one of the places where we do use the word 'cause'. But we also know that this is rather a strange case of causality; the subject is able to give a cause of a thought or feeling or bodily movement in the same kind of way as he is able to state the place of his pain or the position of his limbs. Such statements are not based on observation.

Nor can we say: 'Well, the "reason" for a movement is a cause, and not a reason in the sense of "reason for acting", when the movement is involuntary; it is a reason as opposed to a cause, when the movement is voluntary and intentional'. This is partly because in any case the object of the whole inquiry is really to delineate such concepts as the voluntary and the intentional, and partly because one can also give a 'reason' which is only a 'cause' for what is voluntary and intentional. E.g. 'Why are you walking up and down like that'?— 'It's that military band; it excites me'. Or 'What made you sign the document at last'?—'The thought "It is my duty" kept hammering away in my mind until I said to myself "I can do no other", and so signed'.

Now we can see that the cases where this difficulty arises are just those where the cause itself, *qua* cause, (or perhaps one should rather say the causation itself) is in the class of things known without observation.

I will call the type of cause in question a '*mental cause*'. Mental causes are possible, not only for actions ('The martial music excites me, that is why I walk up and down') but also for feelings and even thoughts. In considering actions, it is important to distinguish between mental causes and motives; in considering feelings, such as fear or anger, it is important to distinguish between mental causes and objects of feeling. To see this, consider the following cases:

A child saw a bit of red stuff on a turn in a stairway and asked what it was. He thought his nurse told him it was a bit of Satan and felt dreadful fear of it. (No doubt she said it was a bit of satin.) What he was frightened of was the bit of stuff; the cause of his fright was his nurse's remark. The object of fear may be the cause of fear, but, as Wittgenstein[1] remarks, is not *as such* the cause of fear. (A hideous face appearing at the window would of course be both cause and object, and hence the two are easily confused.) Or again, you may be angry *at* someone's action, when what makes you angry is some reminder of it, or someone's telling you of it.

[1] *Philosophical Investigations*, § 476.

This sort of cause of a feeling or reaction may be reported by the person himself, as well as recognized by someone else, even when it is not the same as the object. Note that this sort of causality or sense of 'causality' is so far from accommodating itself to Hume's explanations that people who believe that Hume pretty well dealt with the topic of causality would entirely leave it out of their calculations; if their attention were drawn to it they might insist that the word 'cause' was inappropriate or was quite equivocal. Or conceivably they might try to give a Humeian account of the matter as far as concerned the outside observer's recognition of the cause; but hardly for the patient's.

Now one might think that when the question 'Why'? is answered by giving the intention with which a person acts—a case of which I will here simply characterize by saying that it mentions something future—this is also a case of a mental cause. For couldn't it be recast in the form: 'Because I wanted. . .' or 'Out of a desire that. . .'? If a feeling of desire for an apple affects me and I get up and go to a cupboard where I think there are some, I might answer the question what led to this action by mentioning the desire as having made me . . . etc. But it is not in all cases that 'I did so and so in order to . . .' can be backed up by 'I *felt* a desire that . . .' I may e.g. simply hear a knock on the door and go downstairs to open it without experiencing any such desire. Or suppose I feel an upsurge of spite against someone and destroy a message he has received so that he shall miss an appointment. If I describe this by saying 'I wanted to make him miss that appointment', this does not necessarily mean that I had the thought 'If I do this, he will . . . ' and that it affected me with a desire of bringing that about which led up to my action. This may have happened, but need not. It could be that all that happened was this: I read the message, had the thought 'That unspeakable man!' with feelings of hatred, tore the message up, and laughed. Then if the question 'Why did you do that'? is put by someone who makes it clear that he wants me to mention the mental causes—i.e., what went on in my mind and issued in the action—I should perhaps give this account; but normally the reply would be no such thing. That particular inquiry is not very often made. Nor do I wish to say that it always has an answer in cases where it can be made. One might shrug or say 'I don't know that there was any definite history of the kind you mean', or 'It merely occurred to me . . . '

A 'mental cause', of course, need not be a mental event, i.e., a thought or feeling or image; it might be a knock on the door. But if it is not a mental event, it must be something perceived by the person affected—e.g. the knock on the door must be heard—so if in this sense anyone wishes to say it is always a mental event, I have no objection. A mental cause is what someone would describe if he were asked the specific question: what produced this action or thought or feeling in you? i.e., what did you see or hear or feel, or what ideas or images cropped up in your mind, and led up to it? I have isolated this notion of a mental cause because there *is* such a thing as this question with this sort of answer, and because I want to distinguish it from the ordinary senses of 'motive' and 'intention', rather than because it is in itself of very great importance; for I believe that it is of very little. But it is important to have a clear idea of it, partly because *a* very natural conception of 'motive' is that it is what *moves* (the very word suggests that)—glossed as 'what *causes*' a man's actions etc. And 'what causes' them is perhaps then thought of as an event that brings the effect about—though *how*—i.e. whether it should be thought of as a kind of pushing in another medium, or in some other way—is of course completely obscure.

In philosophy a distinction has sometimes been drawn between 'motives' and 'intentions in acting' as referring to quite different things. A man's intention is *what* he aims at or chooses; his motive is what determines the aim or choice; and I suppose that 'determines' must here be another word for 'causes'.

Popularly, 'motive' and 'intention' are not treated as so distinct in meaning. E.g. we hear of 'the motive of gain'; some philosophers have wanted to say that such an expression must be elliptical; gain must be the *intention*, and *desire of gain* the motive. Asked for a motive, a man might say 'I wanted to . . .' which would please such philosophers; or 'I did it in order to . . .' which would not; and yet the meaning of the two phrases is here identical. When a man's motives are called good, this may be in no way distinct from calling his intentions good—e.g. 'he only wanted to make peace among his relations'.

Nevertheless there is even popularly a distinction between the meaning of 'motive' and the meaning of 'intention'. E.g. if a man kills someone, he may be said to have done it out of love and pity, or to have done it out of hatred; these might indeed be cast in the forms 'to release him from this awful suffering', or 'to get rid of the swine'; but though these are forms of expression suggesting objectives, they are perhaps expressive of the spirit in which the man killed rather than descriptive of the end to which the killing was a means—

a future state of affairs to be produced by the killing. And this shows us part of the distinction that there is between the popular senses of motive and intention. We should say: popularly, 'motive for an action' has a rather wider and more diverse application than 'intention with which the action was done'.

When a man says what his motive was, speaking popularly, and in a sense in which 'motive' is not interchangeable with 'intention', he is not giving a 'mental cause' in the sense that I have given to that phrase. The fact that the mental causes were such-and-such may indeed help to make his claim intelligible. And further, though he may say that his motive was this or that one straight off and without lying—i.e. without saying what he knows or even half knows to be untrue—yet a consideration of various things, which may include the mental causes, might possibly lead both him and other people to judge that his declaration of his own motive was false. But it appears to me that the mental causes are seldom more than a very trivial item among the things that it would be reasonable to consider. As for the importance of considering the motives of an action, as opposed to considering the intention, I am very glad not to be writing either ethics or literary criticism, to which this question belongs.

Motives may explain actions to us; but that is not to say that they 'determine', in the sense of causing, actions. We do say: 'His love of truth caused him to . . . ' and similar things, and no doubt such expressions help us to think that a motive must be what produces or brings about a choice. But this means rather 'He did this in that he loved the truth'; it interprets his action.

Someone who sees the confusions involved in radically distinguishing between motives and intentions and in defining motives, so distinct, as the determinants of choice, may easily be inclined to deny both that there is any such thing as mental causality, and that 'motive' means anything but intention. But both of these inclinations are mistaken. We shall create confusion if we do not notice (a) that phenomena deserving the name of mental causality exist, for we can make the question 'Why'? into a request for the sort of answer that I considered under that head; (b) that mental causality is not restricted to choices or voluntary or intentional actions but is of wider application; it is restricted to the wider field of things the agent knows about *not* as an observer, so that it includes some involuntary actions; (c) that motives are not mental causes; and (d) that there is application for 'motive' other than the applications of 'the intention with which a man acts'.

Revenge and gratitude are motives; if I kill a man as an act of revenge I may say I do it in order to be revenged, or that revenge is my object; but revenge is not some further thing obtained by killing him, it is rather that killing him is revenge. Asked why I killed him, I reply 'Because he killed my brother'. We might compare this answer, which describes a concrete past event, to the answer describing a concrete future state of affairs which we sometimes get in statements of objectives. It is the same with gratitude, and remorse, and pity for something specific. These motives differ from, say, love or curiosity or despair in just this way: something that *has happened* (or is at present happening) is given as the ground of an action or abstention that is good or bad for the person (it may be oneself, as with remorse) at whom it is aimed. And if we wanted to explain e.g. revenge, we should say it was harming someone because he had done one some harm; we should not need to add some description of the feelings prompting the action or of the thoughts that had gone with it. Whereas saying that someone does something out of, say, friendship cannot be explained in any such way. I will call revenge and gratitude and remorse and pity backward-looking motives, and contrast them with motive-in-general.

Motive-in-general is a very difficult topic which I do not want to discuss at any length. Consider the statement that one motive for my signing a petition was admiration for its promoter, X. Asked 'Why did you sign it'? I might well say 'Well, for one thing, X, who is promoting it, did . . . ' and describe what he did in an admiring way. I might add 'Of course, I know that is not a ground for signing it, but I am sure it was one of the things that most influenced me'—which need *not* mean: 'I thought explicitly of this before signing'. I say 'Consider this' really with a view to saying 'let us not consider it here'. It is too complicated. The account of motive popularized by Professor Ryle does not appear satisfactory. He recommends construing 'he boasted from vanity' as saying 'he boasted . . . and his doing so satisfies the law-like proposition that whenever he finds a chance of securing the admiration and envy of others, he does whatever he thinks will produce this admiration and envy'.[1] This passage is rather curious and roundabout in its way of putting what it seems to say, but I can't understand it unless it implies that a man could not be said to have boasted from vanity unless he always behaved vainly, or at least very often did so. But this does not seem to be true.

[1] *The Concept of Mind*, p. 89.

To give a motive (of the sort I have labelled 'motive-in-general', as opposed to backward-looking motives and intentions) is to say something like 'See the action in this light'. To explain one's own actions by an account indicating a motive is to put them in a certain light. This sort of explanation is often elicited by the question 'Why'? The question whether the light in which one so puts one's action is a true light is a notoriously difficult one.

The motives admiration, curiosity, spite, friendship, fear, love of truth, despair and a host of others are either of this extremely complicated kind, or are forward-looking or mixed. I call a motive forward-looking if it is an intention. For example, to say that someone did something for fear of . . . often comes to the same as saying he did so lest . . . or in order that . . . should not happen.

Leaving then, the topic of motive-in-general or 'interpretative' motive, let us return to backward-looking motives. Why is it that in revenge and gratitude, pity and remorse, the past event (or present situation) is a reason for acting, not just a mental cause?

Now the most striking thing about these four is the way in which good and evil are involved in them. E.g. if I am grateful to someone, it is because he has done me some good, or at least I think he has, and I cannot show gratitude by something that I intend to harm him. In remorse, I hate some good things for myself; I could not express remorse *by* getting myself plenty of enjoyments, or *for* something that I did not find bad. If I do something out of revenge which is in fact advantageous rather than harmful to my enemy, my action, in its description of being advantageous to him, is involuntary.

These facts are the clue to our present problem. If an action has to be thought of by the agent as doing good or harm of some sort, and the thing in the past as good or bad, in order for the thing in the past to be the reason for the action, then this reason shows not a mental cause but a motive. This will come out in the agent's elaborations on his answer to the question 'Why'?

It might seem that this is not the most important point, but that the important point is that a *proposed* action can be questioned and the answer be a mention of something past. 'I am going to kill him'.— 'Why'?—'He killed my father'. But do we yet know what a proposal to act is; other than a prediction which the predictor justifies, if he does justify it, by mentioning a reason for acting? and the meaning of the expression 'reason for acting' is precisely what we are at present trying to elucidate. Might one not predict mental causes and their effects? Or even their effects after the causes have occurred? E.g.

'This is going to make me angry'. Here it may be worth while to remark that it is a mistake to think one cannot choose whether to act from a motive. Plato saying to a slave 'I should beat you if I were not angry' would be a case. Or a man might have a policy of never making remarks about a certain person because he could not speak about that man unenviously or unadmiringly.

We have now distinguished between a backward-looking motive and a mental cause, and found that here at any rate what the agent reports in answer to the question 'Why'? is a reason-for-acting if, in treating it as a reason, he conceives it as something good or bad, and his own action as doing good or harm. If you could e.g. show that either the action for which he has revenged himself, or that in which he has revenged himself, was quite harmless or beneficial, he ceases to offer a reason, except prefaced by 'I thought'. If it is a proposed revenge he either gives it up or changes his reasons. No such discovery would affect an assertion of mental causality. Whether in general good and harm play an essential part in the concept of intention is something it still remains to find out. So far good and harm have only been introduced as making a clear difference between a backward-looking motive and a mental cause. When the question 'Why'? about a present action is answered by description of a future state of affairs, this is already distinguished from a mental cause just by being future. Here there does not so far seem to be any need to characterize intention as being essentially of good or of harm.

Now, however, let us consider this case:

> Why did you do it?
> Because he told me to.

Is this a cause or a reason? It appears to depend very much on what the action was or what the circumstances were. And we should often refuse to make any distinction at all between something's being a reason and its being a cause of the kind in question; for that was explained as what one is after if one asks the agent what led up to and issued in an action, but being given a reason and accepting it might be such a thing. And how would one distinguish between cause and reason in such a case as having hung one's hat on a peg because one's host said 'Hang up your hat on that peg'? Nor, I think, would it be correct to say that this is a reason and not a mental cause because of the understanding of the words that went into obeying the suggestion. Here one would be attempting a contrast between this case and, say, turning round at hearing someone say Boo! But this case would not in fact be decisively on one side or the other; forced to say whether the noise was a reason or a cause, one would probably decide by how sudden one's reaction was. Further, there is no question of understanding a sentence in the following case: 'Why did you waggle your two fore-fingers by your temples'?—'Because *he* was doing it'; but this is not particularly different from hanging one's hat up because one's host said 'Hang your hat up'. Roughly speaking, if one were forced to go on with the distinction, the more the action is described as a mere response, the more inclined one would be to the word 'cause'; while the more it is described as a response to something as having a *significance* that is dwelt on by the agent, or as a response surrounded with thoughts and questions, the more inclined one would be to use the word 'reason'. But in very many cases the distinction would have no point.

This, however, does not mean that it never has a point. The cases on which we first grounded the distinction might be called 'full-blown'; that is to say, the case of e.g. revenge on the one hand, and of the thing that made me jump and knock a cup off a table on the other. Roughly speaking, it establishes something as a reason to object to it, not as when one says 'Noises should not make you jump like that: hadn't you better see a doctor?' but in such a way as to link it up with motives and intentions. 'You did it because he told you to? But why do what he says?' Answers like 'he has done a lot for me'; 'he is my father'; 'it would have been the worse for me if I hadn't' give the original answer a place among reasons. Thus the full-blown cases are the right ones to consider in order to see the distinction between reason and cause. But it is worth noticing that what is so commonly said, that reason and cause are everywhere sharply distinct notions, is not true.

IX

MOTIVES AND CAUSES

J. O. URMSON

FINDING myself out of sympathy, not merely with the views of my fellow-symposiasts, which would be too common a situation to be worthy of mention, but with their approaches to their problem, I am not in a good position to advance the discussion which they have opened. I propose, therefore, to limit myself to making a few independent comments on our subject, which will show the lines on which I should have liked the problem to have been tackled, and then commenting on the lines of thought pursued by Mr. McCracken and Mr. Peters.

Let us consider some questions which may be asked about an action, at first limiting ourselves to questions which do not contain the puzzling words 'motive' and 'cause'. Leaving aside also the very wide question 'Why did he do that ?', we may start with this list, which makes no claim whatever to completeness:

1. What was the point of his doing that?
2. What was his reason for doing that?
3. What led him to do that?
4. What prompted him to do that?
5. What made him do that?
6. What possessed him to do that?
7. How did he come to do that?
8. How did it come about that he did that?

This list is certainly very incomplete (we can, for example, ask about a person's intentions or purpose) but it is long enough for the purpose which it has to serve. These questions are not perfectly precise, and admit, according to context, of being answered in more than one way; but there are fairly typical types of answer for some of them, and the answers appropriate to some of them would be quite inappropriate as answers to others. Here are some fairly typical examples of such questions with appropriate answers:

From *Proceedings of the Aristotelian Society*, Supp. Vol. 26 (1952). pp. 179–94. Reprinted by courtesy of the author and the Editor of the Aristotelian Society.

1a. *Q.* What was the point of his buying a slow-combustion stove?
     A. To save coal.

2a. *Q.* What was his reason for buying a cheaper model?
     A. He could not afford the better one.

3a. *Q.* What led him to undertake so many offices?
     A. Vanity. (One may also be led, or even spurred, by ambition, or anxiety, or pride.)

4a. *Q.* What prompted him to clean out his desk?
     A. Noticing that his papers were getting dirty.

5a. *Q.* What made him sell on a falling market?
     A. Panic. (Or stupidity.)

6a. *Q.* What possessed him to strike a woman?
     A. Blind fury. (Or ungovernable rage, or an evil demon, possibly.)

7a. *Q.* How did he come to take up the law?
     A. His father was a solicitor.

8a. *Q.* How did it come about that he emigrated?
     A. Well, it is a long story. The Australian Government . . .

Not all these questions have to be answered in the way they are taken to be answered here. For example, the question 'What were his reasons for doing that?' may be understood, as above, as asking what considerations of fact and situation a man had in mind, or else as asking a question much more similar to 'What was the point of his doing that?' But, allowing for this sort of thing, some points none the less emerge from these examples which seem to be worthy of notice.

First of all, it is clear that we can usually ask more than one of these questions of a given action; some of them are complementary, not mutually exclusive. If Mr. Jones buys a slow combustion stove, we may learn that the point was to save coal, that the reason why he chose that particular model was that it was the best that he could afford, that he was prompted to buy it by hearing that Smith had made a great saving in coal by installing one, that it came about because he happened to be in an ironmonger's buying something else when he saw some stoves, etc. On the other hand, some answers to some questions inhibit the asking of some of the other questions; thus, if the answer to question 8 (How did it come about that . . .) is that the agent was compelled by someone else, then it is evident that none of the other questions, not even 'What made him do it?' are appropriate. More importantly for our purposes, an appropriate answer to question 5 (What made him do it?) seems to inhibit a lot of other questions, or, to put the point in another way, a person who thinks that it is appropriate to ask question 5 must think that it is inappropriate to ask some of the other questions. This point must be further explained.

Let us suppose that Jones, in playing chess, moves his Queen into a position where it can be taken by his opponent without return. Someone might ask: 'What made him do that?' If the answer is that he panicked under pressure of time, then the question was appropriate, and no one will think of going on to ask what the point of the move was, or what led Jones to make it. But if the answer is given 'Don't you see, it was the only way of escaping mate in two moves', it would be inappropriate to say, 'Oh, so that is what made him do it'; rather one must say 'Oh, so that was his reason!', or 'So that was the point of it'. In saying this one recognizes that the original question was, in fact, inappropriate to the situation and might have been met with the retort 'Nothing made him do it, for he had a very good reason for it'. When we get the more courteous reply which shows without saying that the original question was inappropriate by, in fact, answering the question which would have been appropriate, we may for convenience call it an incongruous answer. The question, 'What made him do it?' implies that the agent was carried away; that, even if he could give any reasons for acting as he did, mention of them would be superfluous in the explanation of his action, so that we need not ask about reasons, and that to say that the person was led or prompted to act in that way would be too weak. If a congruous answer to that question is given, then, as we have seen, it is confirmed that these other questions are otiose. Because of this we come to use the question 'What made him do it?' sometimes in another, forensic, manner. The questioner may know very well that the agent was not mastered by any impulse, but by asking this question in this way he implies that the action was one for which there could be no good reason, and suggests that some irrational force must have prevailed, though this latter implication is in the circumstances disingenuous. 'What made you do that?' is a question of the same type as 'What possessed you to do that?', differing only by being less vivid. When one is asked such a question in the forensic style one always tries, of course, to give it an incongruous answer which will show the question to be inappropriate;

one will answer as though the question had been 'What were your reasons?', whether one is or is not able to do so convincingly. In general, it is of silly actions that we ask the question in this mocking way. It is of more serious mistakes and misdemeanours that it is asked more seriously. If one asks what made a man commit a crime, then it is implied that he was carried away, and one asks the question of ordinarily respectable people; to ask for his reasons, etc., is to suggest that he is a willing criminal. Of sensible, proper, actions the question is not normally asked at all, since people are supposed to act naturally in that way; to suggest otherwise is possible in the case of, say, unexpected generosity by a miser, but it smacks of the paradoxical combination of perverted principle and weakness of will which Aristotle mentions in the *Nicomachean Ethics*.

The question 'What led him to do that?' seems to be weaker than the questions 'What possessed him?' and 'What made him?', in the sense that it presupposes something less than an inner compulsion; it will therefore combine more easily with other questions. Blind fear, panic, or terror may make one run away in battle. But when a general is led by fear of disaster to refuse battle on favourable terms he need not have lost control of himself, and probably gives out his orders quite intelligently. Ambition may lead one to do things which not everyone would choose to do, but they need not be foolish things, and the situation is different from being mastered by ambition. But to ask what led a man to act in a certain way is to imply that his actions cannot be explained on purely rational grounds, though the additional element may be merely arational rather than irrational. We do not ask what led a chess player to make what was obviously the best move, but may ask what led him to adopt a sound but bold rather than a sound but cautious policy. I hope that it will be a harmless oversimplification to say that in general one is led by non-permanent passions or by traits of character, or idiosyncracies, respectable or otherwise, if one is led at all. Where nothing of this sort is present then the question 'What led him . . . ?' is otiose.

If this were an independent paper, I would go on to say a good deal more about the nature of these questions and their inter-relation, and I would produce more sample questions; that seems to me to be the correct first move in an examination of the nature of motives. But this being the last paper in a symposium, I will be content with one further point on this topic. Suppose that someone goes to a concert in the ordinary way. He does go to concerts. Now there may be a worthwhile answer to the question 'What prompted him to go to this concert?', and no doubt there will be an answer, however trivial, to the question 'How did it come about that he went?' But it would be odd to ask what was the point of his going to the concert if one did not wish to imply that he was not an ordinary concert-goer and, perhaps, hoped to meet Mabel. It would be odd, too, to ask for his reason for going to the concert, or what made him go to the concert, or what led him to go to the concert, though, of course, one might ask such questions if it was the kind of concert that he did not ordinarily go to, or was notoriously going to be very bad. Things like going to concerts, and things like twiddling one's thumbs or going to bed at the usual time, are things of which it would be misleading to ask such questions, in normal circumstances. If we are asked such questions, we must answer that we want to, or like to, which are ways of saying that the question is otiose.

If we consider our original list of questions in the light of these observations, the following points emerge. Firstly, of some actions, which are not mere automatisms, it is misleading to ask for the point, or the reason, or what led, made, possessed the agent so to act. Secondly, where we can ask what made or possessed the agent so to act we cannot ask for his reason, or what led or prompted him to do it. Thirdly, where there is a point or a reason there need not be anything which we can say led or prompted the agent so to act, though there may be. Fourthly, compulsion rules out all these questions, including the question 'What made him do it?', though this latter question may be said to imply an inner compulsion, when not used in the way that I have called forensic.

Now for the point of these considerations which is relevant to my present purpose. The large Oxford English Dictionary defines a motive as follows (omitting irrelevant uses, e.g., the musical one): 'That which "moves" or induces a person to act in a certain way; a desire, fear, or other emotion, or a consideration of reason, which influences or tends to influence a person's volition; also often applied to a contemplated result or object the desire of which tends to influence volition.' Now this, if it were intended as a contribution to philosophy, would no doubt leave much to be desired; but there is surely no complaint to be made from the philological angle. This being so, it is obvious that the question 'What was his motive?' can legitimately be taken to embrace questions about the point of an act (called by the makers of the dictionary the contemplated result), the reason for the act, and also the things (desire, fear, or other emotion) which lead, make, or possess a person to act in a certain way. This is a very mixed bag, and it is surely clear that if we are asked what is the relation of motive to act, without special restrictions on the meaning to be given to the word 'motive', we cannot give a very precise answer, and would be well advised if we did not attempt to give a general answer at all. I take it that Mr. Peters will agree with me on this last point, since he gives a technical sense to 'motive' from the beginning, and will even think that I have been an unnecessarily long time making it. It is, then, I take it, clear that 'What was his motive?' is a question which in its common signification is wide enough to cover most, but not all, of those listed at the beginning of this paper; they may be regarded as more specialized versions of it. It is likely then that before we can hope to gain enlightenment on the nature of motives, we shall have to examine first these more specific questions.

However, there are other questions which we can ask about actions, which are relevant to our present problem. We may ask 'What were his real motives for doing that?' (in the sort of way which does not suggest deliberate deceit), or we may ask 'What were his underlying motives for doing that?' Thus, if Becket in 'Murder in the Cathedral' had not noticed the fourth tempter he might have gone to his death with the real, underlying motive of desire for the 'glory of saints' in the life hereafter, though appearing to himself and to others to act from the very highest sense of duty. We all have to be careful lest envy of our rivals should, without our being aware of it, influence our actions, and so on. Now in the original, comparatively unsophisticated, conception, there is nothing hypothetical or transcendental about these underlying motives. They are more like collar-studs on the carpet than like inaccessible machinery; they may become quite obvious once we notice them. Further, these motives do not *make* us act in a certain way; I may recognize that some unnoticed motive of envy has been unsuccessful in preventing me from recognizing the merits of a rival, and certainly, when we notice them, we may, like Becket, succeed in ridding ourselves of them completely.

Now this straightforward notion of underlying motives appears to have been used for much more sophisticated purposes by the psychoanalytic movement. I am nervous of saying much on a subject which is dangerous even for the expert, but must say a little. One claim that this movement seems to be making is this: that careful, systematic investigation of actions can often reveal hidden, underlying motives which would otherwise have remained hidden and unrealized. That this claim is justified seems to me to be beyond reasonable doubt; it is a claim which is straightforwardly empirical, and which one can corroborate from one's own experience. There also seem to be two other claims made: firstly, that there is always some such hidden motive to be found, that it is never the case that all our motives are immediately evident; secondly, that these underlying motives are of very restricted kinds (sexual, perhaps, or the urge for power), and that these motives are of sole, or at least supreme, importance. Further, a transcendental theory is offered to justify these claims.

It is not my intention, it is beyond my capacity, to confirm or to deny these additional claims which are, or might be, made. I have mentioned them only to bring out the following points. Firstly, that these claims are not logically involved in a recognition that there are sometimes underlying motives for action. Secondly, it is important to observe that here we have an attempt to answer a new question, the question which interests Mr. Peters, though Mr. Peters talks in terms of physiological drives rather than using the conceptions of the analysts. We have now the question 'What were the features of the situation in which the man was, given which we can deduce the action done from certain general propositions?'

Mr. Peters tells us that he does not wish to argue about ordinary usage. He tells us that when we have a general statement and a particular statement which together yield a prediction deductively the general statement is a law, or law-like, and the particular proposition states the cause of the predicted event. Let us, in deference to Mr. Peters' wishes, not argue now whether this is or is not a usual way of using the word 'cause'. Mr. Peters also tells us that '"motive-explanations" proper' are such that from a general statement of the functional dependence of a behaviour sequence on initiating conditions of drive or tension together with a statement of the occurrence of such a drive or tension the action to be explained can be deduced. If we refrain here, also, from arguing about ordinary usage, it is as clear as daylight that motive-explanations are a class of causal explanations. The only point which remains to be settled is whether we have any reason to use the word 'motive' in the way that Mr. Peters uses it, and the answer to this question presumably depends on whether any explanations of actions which are motive-explanations in Mr. Peters' sense can be given which are correct. If they can, then whether or not anyone else calls this sort of explanation an explanation in terms of motives or not, it is clear that it is a very important type of explanation indeed. Whether they can, I do not know; it is a very great pity that Mr. Peters did not choose, or was not able, to give us a genuine example of a motive-explanation of this sort. It seems that Mr. Peters does not give us an example which could claim to be a correct explanation of this type. Surely Mr. Peters does not think that to say that a person stole some apples because he was hungry is to give a correct explanation of this type? Now it is charitable and not unreasonable to believe that 'Hunger *made* him steal the apples' is sometimes true—though anyone who led an adventurous childhood knows that hungry boys sometimes steal apples in situations in which their hunger was far from actually making them steal. Certainly, too, hunger often leads people to steal apples, or prompts them to do it in situations in which original sin and bravado have a lot to do with the matter. But none of these are what Mr. Peters would call a motive-explanation proper. For such there has to be a general statement of functional dependence of behaviour upon drive or tension, from which, together with the occurrence of the drive, the behaviour can be deduced, which is not the case with the more popular sort of explanation we have considered. Does Mr. Peters believe that there is a general proposition from which, together with the initial condition of hunger, we can deduce the stealing of apples? I doubt it. Mr. Peters could not have intended this as a genuine example. It would have been very helpful if Mr. Peters had given us an example of a motive-explanation at least as accurate as his other example: 'Metals expand when heated, and this is a piece of metal'; until he does, all one can say about his view is that it is certain that in his usage of 'cause' and 'motive' motive-explanations are a class of causal explanations; but I for one have not come across any occasions for the use of the word 'motive' in his sense. If, in fact, there are any, then there can be no doubt that his usage is very important.

It is tempting to assimilate Mr. Peters' usage to that of 'What made him do that?' It would, however, be wrong, I think, to do so in a simple-minded way. For Mr. Peters would presumably not wish to deny that there is a difference between what we call hunger making a man steal and hunger leading him to steal, though one gathers that he does not think that these distinctions of unscientific usage are very important, and that somehow his motive-explanation would be possible in both cases. He would not say, then, that all cases of action are really exactly like the case where an overmastering urge makes one do something. On the other hand, if Mr. Peters' sense of 'motive' can be applied to all actions for the motive of which we may ask, we are in that case bound, I think, to regard such distinctions as between being led and being made as of minor interest. On his own views, Mr. Peters is right in being uninterested in these distinctions. This I will now try to show.

Many philosophers have shown recently that the distinction between actions freely done, in the ordinary sense, and such other occurrences as action under compulsion can be stated in such a way that it cannot be obliterated by theoretical philosophical attack. Some, alas, have probably thought, as Prof. Campbell has recently complained, that in showing this they have eliminated the traditional problem of free-will. But, in fact, when the ordinary distinctions have been elucidated, the old problem of free-will merely arises in a new (and, I think, better) dress. As men, whether it falls within the capacity of philosophers to make a further contribution or not, we must now ask: granted that the distinction between free and other actions is plainly feasible, how important is it, how fundamental is it? Is it worth making? Now it seems to me that in rejecting our common-sense distinctions about kinds of motives as unimportant, and accepting as a universal type of motive-explanation something to which an explanation of what made a man act in a certain way is our nearest approach in our ordinary thought, Mr. Peters is coming down to some extent on the side of saying that the free-will and similar distinctions are not worth making, at least when we get out of the street. I say 'to some extent', for Mr. Peters may no doubt think that there is an important distinction between inner drive on the one hand and compulsion from outside and automatisms on the other; but he does seem to me to think that there is no difference in kind between acting under an inner compulsion and other action, in so far as both are brought by him under a single formula of explanation to which Mr. Peters attributes paramount importance. It is indeed possible that Mr. Peters is right in this. But we do not ordinarily think in this way, and Mr. Peters says nothing that I can find to show that he is right and that the single form of explanation which he favours is universally applicable. He himself always talks cautiously of postulated rather than discovered elements in the alleged explanatory statements. I do not say that he is wrong. I only say that it is surprising that he should attribute such overriding importance to a sense of 'motive' which may have no field of application, or, at any rate, a very limited field. To put it another way, it is surprising to me that Mr. Peters should attribute such overwhelming philosophical importance to a usage of 'motive' which has to be attributed to a speculative programme of psychological research which may turn out to be a mistaken programme. Such a programme may be worth pursuing, but we should not make ourselves philosophical hostages to its success. We must not ignore senses of motive in which it is certain that people have motives.

There is one other point, hitherto conceded, on which I must now express doubt concerning Mr. Peters' paper. He says that it is an 'obvious point' that 'to explain an occurrence is to deduce it from general or law-like statements together with initial condition statements describing particular states of affairs. "Efficient causes" only count as explanations of succeeding occurrences if they constitute initial condition statements relative to general assumptions.' We must note that Mr. Peters is not merely claiming that an explanation of that sort can always be given, but that anything which is to count as an explanation at all must always be of that sort. Perhaps Mr. Peters is legislating again without reference to ordinary usage, in which case it would be unprofitable to argue. But if Mr. Peters wishes to claim that what we ordinarily count as an explanation of an occurrence must conform to this pattern, then I think that he is mistaken. Such notions as explanation are not as simple as that. To take an example: a visitor might walk into a debate in Parliament and find the place in an uproar, and ask another spectator for an explanation: 'How did this come about?' The answer might be: 'It was caused quite unpredictably by a completely tame statement by the Minister for This and That.' This would ordinarily count as an explanation of how the uproar came about. Now it might be that the uproar was in fact predictable from some general statement together with the initial condition of a speech of that sort. But this explanation goes out of its way to deny that this is so, and yet would count as an explanation. Perhaps it is not a complete explanation, but that is another question. The point is that we often can give some explanation of an occurrence by saying that this or that caused it when we know of no law of which it is a case, or even think that there is none. Thus, I can be quite certain that it was a speech in Parliament that caused an uproar, without being able to see it as part of a recurrent pattern. If this fits in ill with

Hume's account of causation, that cannot be helped. In the same way it seems that we might explain a man's action by saying that his motive was, say, hunger, without reference, implicit or explicit, to any general statement. The fact that there may be some general statement which is in fact relevant to the explanation is beside the point. To say that there must always be such a general statement relevant is to express one's belief in a certain kind of orderliness, not to analyse explanation, however much the belief may be justified.

When trying to explain human actions we do not often employ the word 'cause'. People so often take *cause* and *make* to be synonymous that, perhaps, it is worth pointing out that when we do ask for the cause of an action we are often asking a very different question from 'What made him do that?' Thus I may ask what caused a person to alter his tactics in circumstances such that there is no suggestion that anything *made* him alter his tactics. 'Who made him do it?' suggests external compulsion; 'What made him do it?' suggests inner compulsion; while 'What caused him to do it?' does neither, though it does not, perhaps, exclude them. On the whole, the most likely candidates as answers to a request for a cause of an action are (in the words of the dictionary) a consideration of reason or some change in the external situation. What, however, does seem abundantly clear is that if we asked 'What caused Jones to do that?' we should feel very surprised, and even cheated, if we received the answer 'Jones himself was the cause of his action' (what would this mean if it is not a mere reiteration of the fact that Jones did it, which we know already?), or if we received the answer that Jones' character caused him to do it. Yet Jones and his character are said by Mr. McCracken to be the fundamental causes of Jones' actions. Mr. McCracken is also very insistent that an aroused motive (as opposed to a motive as a latent disposition) may be a cause of an action. As for Jones and his character being causes of his actions, I find this well-nigh unintelligible, in spite of Mr. McCracken's explanations. But if Mr. McCracken wishes to maintain that, if asked 'What caused Macbeth to abandon his loyalty and murder his king?' a man may properly reply 'His ambition, aroused by the prophecies of the witches, caused him to do it', then I agree that this would be a perfectly proper answer. I agree, too, with Mr. McCracken that it is a mere superstition to think that only an event may be properly named as a cause. It would indeed be absurd in ordinary circumstances to give the fact that a piece of glass has the (ordinary) brittleness of glass as the cause of it breaking; but in ordinary circumstances it would be very proper to mention the (unusual) brittleness of an aircraft's wing as the cause of the wing falling off, and quite ridiculous to mention the fact that wind was pressing against the wing in quite a normal way, if investigating the cause of an accident.

But Mr. McCracken wants to go further than this. He seems to think that it is necessary to hold that motives are causes if we are to attribute to them a true importance; that it is somehow to belittle motives to deny that they are causes. This seems odd to me. Let us admit for the moment that we can always give a motive by using such a formula as 'this caused him to act like that'; yet it seems that this is only a tribute to the extraordinary imprecision of the notion of cause, and in no way a vindication of the reality or importance of motives. If a motive is to be said to cause me to act in a certain way, equally the typical artistic insensitivity of the average interior decorator may be said to cause me to act in a certain way or to become depressed. If we give up the dogma that causes must be hard events, then we must give up the connected dogma of the peculiar hardness of causes with it, and no longer think that to say that something was a cause is necessarily to attribute to it any special degree of metaphysical hardness.

I am then willing to agree with Mr. McCracken that motives may be called causes, simply because to ask for a cause is to ask such a very general question that practically anything of any kind may be mentioned in an answer. His alternative sort of argument for this position does not appeal to me. He says: Macbeth's ambition was his motive; his ambition caused many deaths; therefore motives are a species of causes. This seems to me to be like the argument: Macbeth's cousin was his best friend; his cousin was a Scot; therefore best friends are a species of Scot. What this sort of argument shows is that what is referred to in one context as a best friend may be referred to in another as a Scot, and that what is referred to in one context as a motive may be referred to in another as a cause. And this is not what Mr. McCracken wishes to show, or not all of it.

Having been unconciliatory to both my fellow-symposiasts, I must end on the same carping note with regard to the title of this symposium. It is without doubt a problem of importance which is being posed when we are asked to discuss the nature of motives. But it seems to be a barren approach to the problem to ask whether motives are causes. This is so for two reasons. Firstly, it is not the right approach to ask questions straight away about the nature of motives in general; it is essential to see first what more specific questions can be asked. When we see how many and how different specific questions are covered, as the dictionary on its own can make us see, it becomes doubtful whether anything useful can be said about motives in general, and in any case abundantly clear that in any case before we attempt any generalizations, a careful study of the more specific questions is necessary. Secondly, if we are to ask general questions about motives, to ask whether they are causes is not a helpful one. It is not helpful because when we have said yes or no we have said so little. We, in fact, use the word 'cause' quite rarely in our explanation of actions, but to a request for a cause practically any answer which gives any enlightenment may be given. Only by an artificial narrowing down of the notion of a cause can the question be made useful; and it is not desirable to have to narrow one's questions down artificially before they can be answered. That field has been extensively cultivated by philosophers and has been found to be very infertile.

It seems to me that we should not try to answer such questions as 'Are motives causes?' but should rather ask questions like 'What is it to have a reason for acting in a certain way?'; 'What is it to be led by ambition to do so and so?'; 'What is it to be driven by fear to do this or that?'; 'What is the difference between being driven and being led by anxiety?'; 'Can what merely prompts one be called a motive?' and so on. No doubt an examination of the specialized use by psychologists of the notion of motive also has a proper place, though I see no reason for giving it pre-eminence, among these questions. It is only by this piecemeal approach that anything permanent can be achieved; though no doubt it is an unspectacular and pedestrian procedure. But the end of a third paper is not the place to start on this exacting task.

NOTES ON THE CONTRIBUTORS

J. L. AUSTIN, who died in 1960, was White's Professor of Moral Philosophy at Oxford from 1952, and previously a Fellow of Magdalen College. After his death there were published his *Philosophical Papers* (1961), *Sense and Sensibilia* (1962), and *How to Do Things with Words* (1962).

ARTHUR C. DANTO is a member of the Department of Philosophy at Columbia University. His book *Nietzsche as Philosopher* appeared in 1965, and *Analytical Philosophy of Knowledge* in 1968.

H. A. PRICHARD, who died in 1947, was White's Professor of Moral Philosophy at Oxford from 1928 to 1937. His major writings were collected by Sir David Ross in the two volumes *Moral Obligation* (1949) and *Knowledge and Perception* (1950).

A. I. MELDEN is a member of the Department of Philosophy at the University of California at Irvine. His *Rights and Right Conduct* appeared in 1959, and *Free Action* in 1961.

DONALD DAVIDSON is a member of the Department of Philosophy at Princeton University. His book *Decision Making: an Experimental Approach* (with P. Suppes) appeared in 1957.

JOEL FEINBERG is a member of the Department of Philosophy at Rockefeller University. He has published several papers in philosophical periodicals, and has edited *Moral Concepts* in this series.

P. J. FITZGERALD is now Professor of Law at the University of Kent at Canterbury, and was formerly a Fellow of Trinity College, Oxford. His *Criminal Law and Punishment* appeared in 1962.

G. E. M. ANSCOMBE is Professor of Philosophy, Cambridge. Among her writings are *Intention* (1957), *Introduction to Wittgenstein's Tractatus* (1959), and *Three Philosophers* (with P. T. Geach, 1961).

J. O. URMSON is a Fellow of Corpus Christi College, Oxford, and was formerly Professor of Philosophy at Dundee. His book *Philosophical Analysis* was published in 1958, and he edited the late J. L. Austin's William James lectures, *How to Do Things with Words*.

BIBLIOGRAPHY

(not including material in this volume)

General

1 D'ARCY, E., *Human Acts* (Clarendon Press, Oxford, 1963).
2 HAMPSHIRE, S., *Thought and Action* (Chatto and Windus, London, 1959), esp. chs. 2–3.
3 ——*Freedom of the Individual* (Chatto and Windus, London, 1965).
4 KENNY A., *Action, Emotion and Will* (Routledge and Kegan Paul, London, 1963).
5 MELDEN, A. I., *Free Action* (Routledge and Kegan Paul, London, 1961).
6 MORRIS, H. (ed.), *Freedom and Responsibility* (Stanford U.P., Stanford, 1961).
7 PEARS, D. F. (ed.), *Freedom and the Will* (Macmillan, London, 1963).
8 TAYLOR, C., *The Explanation of Behaviour* (Routledge and Kegan Paul, London, 1964).

The Nature of Action

9 ACKRILL, J. L., 'Aristotle's Distinction between Energeia and Kinesis', *New Essays on Plato and Aristotle*, ed. R. Bambrough (Routledge and Kegan Paul, London, 1965).
10 ARISTOTLE: see *Index Aristotelicus*, ed. H. Bonitz (Graz, 1955) under Energeia, Kinesis, Pathos, Poiesis, Praxis.
11 AUSTIN, J., *Lectures on Jurisprudence* (London, 1863): Lectures XVIII–XIX.
12 BAIER, K., 'Acting and Producing', *Journal of Philosophy*, LXII (1965), 645–48.
13 ——'Action and Agent', *Monist*, 49 (1965), 183–95.
14 CHISHOLM, R. M., 'The Descriptive Element in the Concept of 'Action', *Journal of philosophy*, LXI (1964), 613–24.
15 DANTO, A. C., 'What we can do', *Journal of Philosophy*, LX (1963), 435–45.
16 DAVENEY, T. F., 'Choosing', *Mind*, LXXIII (1964), 515–26.
17 DIAS, R. W. M., *Jurisprudence* (Butterworth, London, 1964), ch. 10.
18 EWING, A. C., 'What is Action?', *Proceedings of the Aristotelian Society*, Suppl. XVII (1938), 86–101.

19 FRANKS, O. S., 'What is Action?', *Proceedings of the Aristotelian Society,* Suppl. XVII (1938), 102–20.

20 GEACH, P. T., 'Ascriptivism', *The Philosophical Review,* LXIX (1960), 221–5.

21 HAMLYN, D. W., 'Behaviour', *Philosophy,* XXVIII (1953), 132–45.

22 HART, H. L. A., 'The Ascription of Responsibility and Rights', *Proceedings of the Aristotelian Society,* XLIX (1949), 171–94.

23 HOBBES, J., *Leviathan* (1651) esp. Part I, ch. 6.

24 HOLMES, O. W., *The Common Law* (MacMillan, London, 1911), ch. 2.

25 HUME, D., *A Treatise of Human Nature* (1738), esp. Book II, part iii, §§ 1–4.

26 ———, *An Enquiry Concerning Human Understanding* (1748), §§ vii–viii.

27 KOTARBINSKI, T., 'Concept of Action', *Journal of Philosophy,* LVII (1960), 215–22.

28 LADD, J., 'The Ethical Dimensions of the Concept of Action', *Journal of Philosophy,* LXII (1965), 633–45.

29 LOCKE, J., *An Essay Concerning Human Understanding* (1690), Book II, ch. xxi.

30 MacMURRAY, J., 'What is Action?', *Proceedings of the Aristotelian Society,* Suppl. XVII (1938), 69–85.

31 MILL, J. S., *System of Logic* (1843), Book III, ch. v, § 11.

32 O'SHAUGHNESSY, B., 'The Limits of the Will', *The Philosophical Review,* LXV (1956), 443–90.

33 PALMER, F. R., *A Linguistic Study of the English Verb* (Longmans, London, 1965).

34 PARSONS, T. and SHILS, E. A. (eds.), *Towards a general theory of Action* (Harvard U. P., Camb. Mass, 1951).

35 PENNOCK, J. R., 'The Problem of Responsibility', in *Responsibility, Nomos III,* ed. C. J. Friedrich (Liberal Arts Press, New York, 1960), 3–27.

36 PITCHER, G., 'Hart on Action and Responsibility', *The Philosophical Review,* LXIX (1960), 226–35.

37 POTTS, T. C., 'States, Activities and Performances', *Proceedings of the Aristotelian Society,* Suppl. XXXIX (1965), 65–84.

38 RYLE, G., *The Concept of Mind,* (Hutchinson, London, 1949), chs. 3–4.

39 SACHS, D., 'A few morals about Acts', *The Philosophical Review,* LXXV (1966), 91–98.

40 SILBER, J. R., 'Human Action and the Language of Volitions', *Pro-*

ceedings of the Aristotelian Society, LXIV (1964), 199–220.

41 TAYLOR, C. C. W., 'States, Activities and Performances', *Proceedings of the Aristotelian Society*, Suppl. XXXIX (1965), 85–102.

42 TAYLOR, R., 'I can', *The Philosophical Review*, LXIX (1960), 78–89.

43 VENDLER, Z., 'Verbs and Times', *The Philosophical Review*, LXVI (1957), 143–160.

44 VESEY, G. N. A., 'Volition', *Philosophy*, XXXVI (1961), 352–65.

45 WILLIAMS, G. L., *Criminal Law. The General Part* (Stevens, London, 1961), ch. 1.

46 WITTGENSTEIN, L., *Philosophical Investigations* (Blackwell, Oxford, 1953), § § 611–60.

Descriptions of Action

47 ANSCOMBE, G. E. M., 'On brute facts', *Analysis*, 18 (1958), 69–72.

48 ———, 'The two kinds of error in Action', *Journal of Philosophy*, LX (1963), 393–401.

49 AUSTIN, J. L., *How to do Things with Words* (Clarendon Press, Oxford, 1962).

50 BENNETT, J., 'Whatever the Consequences', *Analysis*, 26 (1966), 83–102.

51 BENSON, J., 'The Characterisation of Actions and the Virtuous Agent', *Proceedings of the Aristotelian Society*, LXIII (1963), 251–66.

52 BENTHAM, J., *The Principles of Morals and Legislation* (Oxford, 1789), esp. chs. vii–x.

53 CHOPRA, Y. N., 'The Consequences of Human Actions', *Proceedings of the Aristotelian Society*, LXV (1965), 147–66.

54 DONNELLAN, K. S., 'Knowing what I am doing', *Journal of Philosophy*, LX (1963), 401–9.

55 GRIFFIN, J., 'Consequences', *Proceedings of the Aristotelian Society*, LXV (1965), 167–82.

56 MEILAND, J. W., 'Are there Unintentional Actions?', *The Philosophical Review*, LXXII (1963), 377–81.

57 WILL, F. L., 'Intention, Error and Responsibility', *Journal of Philosophy*, LXI (1964), 171–9.

Explanations of Action

58 ANSCOMBE, G. E. M., *Intention* (Blackwell, Oxford, 1957).

59 AUSTIN, J. L., 'Three ways of spilling ink', *The Philosophical Review*, LXXV (1966), 427–40.

60 AYER, A. J., *Man as a Subject for Science*, Auguste Comte Memorial Lecture 6 (Athlone Press, London 1964).

61 BAIER, K., 'Reasons for doing something', *Journal of Philosophy*, LXI (1964), 198–203.

62 BECK, L. W., 'Agent, Actor, Spectator and Critic', *Monist*, 49 (1965), 167–82.

63 ——, 'Conscious and Unconscious Motives', *Mind*, LXXV (1966), 155–79.

64 BENNETT, D., 'Action, Reason and Purpose', *Journal of Philosophy*, LXII (1965), 85–96.

65 BEROFSKY, B., 'Determinism and the Concept of a person', *Journal of Philosophy*, LXI (1964), 461–75.

66 BRANDT, R. and KIM, J., 'Wants as Explanations of Actions', *Journal of Philosophy*, LX (1963), 425–35.

67 BRODBECK, May, 'Meaning and Action', *Philosophy of Science*, 30 (1963), 309–24.

68 BROWN, R., 'The Explanation of Behaviour', *Philosophy*, XL (1965), 344–8.

69 GOLDBERG, B. 'Can a desire be a cause?', *Analysis*, 25 (1965), 70–72.

70 HAMLYN, D. W., 'Causality and Human Behaviour', *Proceedings of the Aristotelian Society*, Suppl. XXXVIII (1964), 125–42.

71 HART, H. L. A. and HONORÉ, A. M., *Causation in the Law* (Clarendon Press, Oxford, 1959).

72 HART, H. L. A., 'Acts of Will and Responsibility', *Jubilee Lectures at Sheffield*, ed. O. R. Marshall (Stevens, London, 1960), 115–44.

73 HEATH, P. L., 'Intentions', *Proceedings of the Aristotelian Society*, Suppl. XXIX (1955), 147–64.

74 JENKINS, J. S., 'Motives and Intention', *The Philosophical Quarterly*, 15 (1965), 155–64.

75 LOUCH, A. R., 'Science and Psychology', *British Journal for the Philosophy of Science*, 12 (1962), 314–27.

76 MACINTYRE, A. C., 'A Mistake about Causality in Social Science', *Philosophy, Politics and Sociology*, II, ed. P. Laslett and W. G. Runciman (Blackwell, Oxford, 1962), 48–70.

77 ——'The Antecedents of Action', *British Analytical Philosophy*, ed. Williams and Montefiore, (Routledge and Kegan Paul, London, 1966) 205–25.

78 PASSMORE, J. A., 'Intentions', *Proceedings of the Aristotelian Society*, Suppl. XXIX (1955), 131–46.

79 PETERS, R. S., *The Concept of Motivation* (Routledge and Kegan Paul, London, 1958).

80 PETERS, R. S. and TAJFEL, H., 'Hobbes and Hull—Metaphysicians of Behaviour', *British Journal for the Philosophy of Science*, VII (1957), 30–44.

81 SCHEFFLER, I., *The Anatomy of Inquiry* (Knopf, New York, 1963), 88–123.

82 SMART, J. J. C., 'Causality and Human Behaviour', *Proceedings of the Aristotelian Society*, Suppl. XXXVIII (1964), 143–8.

83 SUTHERLAND, N. S., 'Motives as Explanations', *Mind*, LXVIII (1959), 145–59.

84 TEICHMANN, J., 'Mental Cause and Effect', *Mind*, LXX (1961), 36–52.

85 WHITE, A. R., *The Philosophy of Mind* (Random House, New York, 1967), ch. 6.

INDEX OF NAMES

(not including authors mentioned only in the Bibliography)